# A Year in the Countryside

## with Rosemary Tilbrook

Edited by
Valerie Macfarlane

With pictures by
Richard Tilbrook

Red Squirrels Publishing

# EDITOR'S NOTE

*W*ALKING with Rosemary was always a delight. One got a botany lesson whether asked for or not – any conversation could be interrupted, nothing was sacrosanct. Looking back over the many happy hours spent walking and naturalising with her and reading through all her 'In the Countryside' articles – some 1200 in all, written for the *Eastern Daily Press* from 1987 until her death in 1999 – I catch a glimpse of her bending over an exciting find or hear her wonderful spontaneous laugh at the discovery of something unexpected. For me, Rosemary is not just a memory of a very dear friend – she lives in every word – and her special ability to penetrate the very soul of the natural world has heightened my own perception of all that I see around me.

In making the selection for this, the first, volume of her work, I, as editor, have made several arbitrary and personal decisions based on my knowledge of Rosemary's own special interests.

The book is divided into seasons, but not strictly according to our interpretation of the calendar, but rather, as to how we perceive events throughout the year – and anyway, the natural world behaves according to its own calendar with little regard for the horological measurement imposed by man. Accordingly, things we associate with Spring, Summer, Autumn, Winter, have been placed in those categories according to our expectations of them – regardless of the havoc wrought by global warming, etc!

Similarly, the articles are in no way chronological but arranged to – hopefully – maximise interest. They are as eclectic in their selection as was Rosemary's far-reaching interest in the natural world and start with her very first article on a flower she adored – the common daisy: 'Daisy, Daisy' of 21st October 1986.

The dates given are the published dates and although this selection relates predominately to the Norfolk countryside the reader will detect some occasional straying over the border into neighbouring Suffolk.

I have tried to correctly identify the subjects of all the illustrations but any failure in this respect must remain mine alone. Editing the original text has been kept to the minimum but where it has been necessary, I have tried to preserve that which was essentially 'Rosemary'.

Rosemary's articles generated an enormous response from her readers who came from all walks of life and furnished her with a constant supply of interesting material. She made many valuable friendships within the natural history world and she would certainly want their important contribution to be acknowledged here with heartfelt thanks.

If Rosemary had a message to leave us it could well have been: "Cherish the natural world and look at it in wonder."

Valerie Macfarlane, *Editor*

ISBN 0-9538946-0-6
© Red Squirrels Publishing, 2000

*Published by Red Squirrels Publishing*
*Designed by Mike Fuggle and printed by EAE Ltd*

# CONTENTS

| | |
|---|---|
| *Introduction* | *page* v |

## Spring

| | |
|---|---|
| Daisy, Daisy! | 2 |
| Held in an icy spell | 3 |
| Countryside thoughts | 4 |
| Loveliness of the fair maids of February | 5 |
| Shy star of woodland | 6 |
| Nature on the move | 7 |
| Fascination of fungi | 8 |
| Spectacle and secrets of Spring's welcome harbingers | 9 |
| Tasselled beauty | 10 |
| Alder catkins | 11 |
| Out with a bat expert | 12 |
| Valuable ivy | 13 |
| A snowdrop pilgrimage | 14 |
| The brave beetle | 16 |
| Pussy willows | 17 |
| Butter-yellow heralds | 18 |
| A special place for mothing | 19 |
| Gilding the churchyards | 20 |
| Early primroses | 21 |
| Flight of the 'Fairy Bees' | 22 |
| First fine haze of hawthorn | 23 |
| Spangles of spilt gold | 24 |
| Shakespeare's flower returns | 25 |
| Opening each-others eyes | 26 |

## Summer

| | |
|---|---|
| Looking at life along a little lane | 28 |
| Mists of muffled bells | 29 |
| All quiet after frog's amorous frenzies | 30 |
| Foaming Queen of the meadow | 31 |
| A wildlife walk | 32 |
| Explosion of colour | 33 |
| Webbed feet in the market place | 34 |
| Gilding the grassy places | 35 |
| Majestic architecture | 36 |
| Wonder of white | 37 |
| Enchantment in the dark | 38 |
| Pretty woodland flowers | 39 |
| Dandelion gold | 40 |
| Perfection of a hidden nest | 41 |

| | |
|---|---|
| Roses | 42 |
| Night air is filled with a sweet smell | 44 |
| Raucous music of rooks | 45 |
| Horsey Mere | 46 |
| An amazing life story | 47 |
| The call of the wild | 48 |
| Foxglove's magic | 49 |
| Who will listen to the hedgerow's lament? | 50 |
| Orange-tip a late spring beauty | 51 |
| This other Eden | 52 |
| Legends of a flower you can't forget | 53 |
| Brief escape into wilderness | 54 |
| Spires and chalices | 55 |
| Floral purple prose passages | 56 |
| Starry native of damp woods | 58 |

## Autumn

| | |
|---|---|
| Woodland walk | 60 |
| Fairy-like fungi | 61 |
| Beauty of butterflies | 62 |
| Monster Lobster Moth looks like dead leaves | 63 |
| A walk in the wilderness | 64 |
| Strolling across fen is always a delight | 65 |
| Song on the wing | 66 |
| Flowers by the sea | 67 |
| Amazing world of wild birds | 68 |
| A Hornet's nest | 69 |
| Discover a wildlife gem | 70 |
| Hopalong insects | 72 |
| Magic appeal of Mouse's home | 73 |
| Adventure of Betty Beetle | 74 |
| Flower Power against the flea menace | 75 |
| Sexton Beetles | 76 |
| Stiffkey saltmarsh | 77 |
| Meadow lament | 78 |
| Babbling brook | 79 |
| Havens of wildlife in our verges | 80 |
| Amazing mechanism's | 82 |
| Nature's clocks | 83 |
| A fragrant, feathery bedstraw | 84 |
| Melancholy beauty | 85 |
| Wild orchids | 86 |
| Morning glory is a hedgerow delight | 87 |
| Acorns by the ton | 88 |

## Winter

| | |
|---|---|
| Plenty of clues for woodland detectives | 90 |
| Small coppers find their way | 91 |
| Delightful ramble down by the river | 92 |
| Beautiful wayside flower | 93 |
| Butterfly is brilliantly disguised as a dead leaf | 94 |
| Magical colours | 95 |
| Feathered ballet | 96 |
| Mysterious world inside a delightful 'pincushion' | 97 |
| Churchyard lichens | 98 |
| Harvest of the hedgerows | 99 |
| Good times with old friends | 100 |
| Sparham pools | 102 |
| Clash of colours is an annual delight | 103 |
| The untouchables | 104 |
| Nature's colourful necklaces are a joy | 105 |
| Furry caterpillars | 106 |
| Old Man's Beard | 107 |
| Holly was Roman introduction | 108 |
| Mistletoe – the Druid healer | 109 |
| Useful plant to scare goblins | 110 |
| A barn owl surveys its territory | 111 |
| Christmas violets | 112 |
| *Index* | 113 |

# ROSEMARY TILBROOK
# WRITER AND NATURALIST

ROSEMARY began writing her "In the Countryside" articles for the EDP in 1986 and by the time of her death had written some twelve hundred. Together they form a beautiful calendar of the seasons and cover every aspect of the complex life of the wild things that make our English countryside such a joy.

Rosemary was initiated into the study of natural history as a little girl while on nature walks with her school teacher mother. She never lost this childlike wonder and it seemed to me, when I accompanied her on her nature walks, that she actually entered into the very life of the flower or insect she was studying. It was this intense, almost childlike empathy, that gave her writing its unique flavour. Other people wrote about the same things as Rosemary but no one in quite the same way. There is some quality about Rosemary's imagery that captures the very essence of her subject. Her articles carry a special "Rosemary Tilbrook" style that is always recognisable.

Rosemary was brought up in Staffordshire and came to Norwich in the early fifties, when we married, eventually setting up home in a Tudor cottage in Ashwellthorpe inhabited at the time by a large family of red squirrels (all of them individually named by Rosemary) and it was from this idyllic setting that Rosemary created her articles. They began as pencilled notes in a notebook or sometimes descriptions breathed into a pocket tape recorder. A first draft was typed on an old electric typewriter before the final perfect copy followed. Rosemary spurned the word processor and the fax machine and every single article had to be delivered in a great rush to Prospect House (usually by me) in order to meet a tight deadline.

Apart from her writing Rosemary became very absorbed in the life of her village and was chairman of the Parish Council up to the time of her death. She was also a councillor with South Norfolk for over thirty years, eventually becoming chairman.

In character Rosemary was as fearless and determined as she was honest and fought hard for what she believed. She was immensely popular with all lovers of the countryside and had a great following. She also had a fine sense of humour coupled with an infectious laugh. A particular transgression to her was the ruthless habit of cutting verges and destroying wild flowers and the habitats of wild creatures. Beautifully manicured churchyards were also anathema to her. A favourite word of Rosemary's was "wilderness" and she would dearly have liked to put the clock back to a time before insecticides and fertilisers to a Thomas Hardy England.

It is a great joy to me to know that Rosemary's special vision of the English countryside should be permanently preserved in a book. The wildlife of our English countryside may, sadly, be on the decline and Rosemary's nostalgia for a pre industrial England can, unfortunately never come to pass but certain things do remain unchanged. A dandelion will always be a dandelion and Rosemary's description of them as "shaggy suns" will always bring them alive to me. I am proud that my camera was able to play a small part in her work as, lying on my stomach and struggling to interpret her often impossible demands, was never easy. But Rosemary was a perfectionist and the world of nature was sacred to her.

I like to think that Rosemary may, in time to come, be considered the Gilbert White of her day and I believe that her writings will never lose their freshness. This book contains only a tiny percentage of her work. Let us hope that others may follow.

*Richard Tulloch*

# Spring

When Daisies pied, and Violets blue,
And Ladiesmocks all silver white,
And Cuckoo-buds of yellow hue,
Do paint the meadows with delight

Loves Labour's Lost<br>Act 5th. Scene 2nd.

# DAISY, DAISY!

*D*AISIES – dear little bright-eyed things – are the commonest of all our sweet wild flowers, and they grow scattered about in grassy places almost everywhere. For many of us they were the first flowers of childhood, and much cherished for making necklaces and daisy-chains. I believe it was Swinburne who said that cutting flowers and sticking them in vases was a barbarous practice.

Today I feel that the daisy-chains of my childhood were a slightly barbarous practice, too! For who would have a primrose chain, or necklaces from wild orchids?

I have just been examining a milky way of daisies in the garden, deliberately unmown because I love them so. Common things can be so beautiful because they are common.

The name "daisy" is a contraction of "day's eye" because when the day is bright the flower is wide open, resembling a small sun.

When the day is grey and cloudy the daisy rays become appealingly cupped with the little sun deep in the bottom. And when the light begins to fail at the end of the day the daisy closes and it is then that one notices the dear little toothed green cup at the back of the head. I have always felt that daisies are at their most appealing when their rays are irresistibly tipped with crimson.

Chaucer wrote about daisies with great affection, and Spencer, Shakespeare, Wordsworth and Burns wrote about them, too. I often think how long-suffering daisies are beneath our feet, and how badly we behave towards them.

We are so big and they are so small. We tread on them unthinkingly. We mow them down by the thousand – and up they come again! Daisies are in flower, unlike most other plants, nearly all the year round. They are charming and innumerable, one of the sweetest of all our wild flowers, and their home is everywhere. We take great care not to tread on the primroses and the violets. But how many people take any care at all not to tread on the daisies!

*21 October 1986*

Common Daisy *Bellis perennis*

# HELD IN AN ICY SPELL

RECENTLY, during the dusky light of dawn and the strange silence of a countryside blanketed with snow, I was surprised to hear the tuning-up of the dawn chorus.

The darkness was suddenly pierced by the silvery strains of a robin, followed by blackbirds with rousing clarions of repetitive chinking, one blackbird's voice setting off another with startling intensity.

The cheepy chatter of sparrows, the soothing sounds of a wood-pigeon, rough cawing of rooks in the distance and the metallic saw-sharpening of a great tit gradually greeted the coming of the day.

The robin's song in the dissolving darkness with its plaintive trickle of notes was a little thing of great beauty.

During the frost-biting dark of the night, holly leaves had become rimmed along their wavy edges with rime, dead stems of willowherb feathered with icy spicules, and there were needles of frost on the stinging nettles.

Bramble leaves were encrusted with sparkling frost crystals, and the hogweed heads, whose umbels had been clotted with snowballs, were exquisitely crystallized as though dredged with sugar.

The sloping springy branches of a fir tree were coated with a fairy kind of beauty no oak or ash could ever attain. The lime green of the algal bloom, powdering tree trunks and branches everywhere, was prettily enhanced by the whiteness of the snow.

Groups of icicles, tapering and spiky, were hanging from a honeysuckle against a cottage wall. How beautiful is the pendent freezing of dripping water, light-shot and glistening like glassy stalactites. The frail beauty of snowflakes coming to rest, the intricacies of frost crystals with lacy structures, twigs glazed with ice, and leaves rimed with "frost flowers" distilled from the damp of the night – have a magical power to delight.

For a fleeting moment, such fugitive beauty catches the eye and holds the mind with its icy spell.

*24 February 1991*

'glazed twigs and frost flowers'

# COUNTRYSIDE THOUGHTS

*I* was thinking the other day what an enormous debt we owe to those who love wildlife, and are anxious about its world.

Those who are authors and broadcasters, who make stunningly beautiful films for television, and who have opened the eyes of millions to the awesome responsibility we all share of looking after what is left of the world of the wild with its aching need, whether in the tropical rain forests, or our own little patch of the Norfolk countryside.

The world of the wild is the love of my life, and the influences on me, by those who have walked the way of the wild in Norfolk and elsewhere, have been enormous.

Some have opened my eyes, opened windows in the the mind, lit a candle there that will never go out.

My mother, who taught natural history, laid a foundation stone in the ground of my being, where wild things were concerned, and Beatrix Potter – a powerful formative influence in childhood – cemented it in.

The countryside in those days was leafy and lovely, and not the shattering disillusion it so often is today.

One of the great wildlife milestones in my life was meeting Romany and Raq who came from a world that can never be recaptured.

The grief when he died, and his BBC nature talks ended for ever, was dreadful for thousands of listeners all over Britain. Gavin Maxwell's remote and hauntingly lonely life in the wilds of Scotland was another milestone, and the verbal magic of his books enchanted the imagination of thousands of readers.

Bronowski and Carl Sagan with their superb teaching on television expanded one's understanding about the cosmos right down to the libraries contained in a single living cell. All of these human influences, both great and small, have been moulding and enlightening, for which one is eternally thankful.

Norfolk's own countryside writers have spirited me away for weeks on end into previous centuries, especially the late E.A.E., whose thoughts and feelings resonated inside so many of us, every morning for nearly 40 years.

How glad I am that I was born at the right time. Glad that I have lived through a golden age of wildlife, where little lanes were irreplaceably beautiful.

*13 February 1987*

# LOVELINESS OF THE
# FAIR MAIDS OF FEBRUARY

*T*ODAY I have been looking at snowdrops, single ones, flowering in local churchyards. How elegant and simple they are in outline. They rise from the ground like white-tipped spears, and then, among sea-green leaves, they curve over, and chaste and beautiful they form "drops of snow".

There are tens of thousands of snowdrops at Walsingham Abbey, the Old Rectory at Holt, and in the wood beside the medieval Greyfriars' Priory at Dunwich, where they flower against its 13th century wall and beside the sea.

Snowdrops, a name so echoing the natural beauty of the flowers themselves, were once rare in Britain. Though possibly native in damp woods in western England, for the most part they are thought to have been introduced to this country by the Romans. Wherever they originated, our fair maids of February, as they are sometimes called, are very much at home in wild places here in Norfolk and Suffolk.

It is curious that many snowdrops occur in Britain on monastic sites. Perhaps the monks of the Middle Ages on their visits to Rome brought back snowdrops for use as emblems of purity on Candlemas Day, the Feast of the Purification of the Virgin.

For there was a time when statues of the Virgin Mary were removed from their altars and snowdrops strewn in the vacant places; and processions in churches included girls robed in white, carrying snowdrops.

There is a very beautiful legend about the Fall of Man after which snow covered the earth with a white pall. Eve was weeping bitterly, for in the barrenness outside "The Garden", all was desolate. No flower grew anywhere. Hope seemed dead. Then an angel, who appeared and comforted Eve, caught a flake of falling snow and breathed on it – thus the first snowdrop was born.

The snowdrops I looked at today were diffusing a sweet, honeyed scent among their spreading sepals. The inner petals were charm itself, and like the daintiest of petticoats. For they were marked with many green striations bearing nectar on their insides and tipped with green along their scalloped edges on the outside. Enclosed within each was a long green style encircled by orange stamens.

How pretty are all the details of the snowdrop, which we rarely, if ever, examine closely.

*26 January 1998*

Snowdrop *Galanthus nivalis*

# SHY STAR OF WOODLAND

*How* delightful are the wood anemones at the moment, flowering above leaf litter, like earth-bound stars on the woodland floors.

Of the greatest delicacy and beauty, how fragile-looking are these nodding little flowers of spring when buffeted by the roughness of the wind, wind-flowers, of course, being another of their names.

There is a charming legend concerning the wood anemone which describes Venus wandering through woodland weeping for the death of her lover, Adonis. Where her tears have dropped – the windflower blows.

These dainty flowers which range from pure white to faintly flushed with mauve or more strikingly, tinged with reddish-purple do not have true petals. In fact they have a whorl of petal-like sepals which have taken on the role of petals. In the middle of the flower there is a green fruiting head consisting of numerous carpels (divisions of the ovary), which is eventually transformed into a globe-shaped cluster of downy fruits. Encircling the fruiting head there is a delightful and delicate fringe of stamens with golden-yellow anthers.

Wood anemones, which belong to the buttercup or Ranunculaceae family, have no nectaries but are visited by bees and beetles for their pollen. If the weather is sunny the flowers are open, their heads uplifted and star-like; if the weather is cloudy or rain threatens the flowers, or if it is near the evening, they close and become gracefully bell-like to protect their pollen.

The leaves are as beautiful as the flowers. They are formed in an adorning whorl of three, deeply-cut and ferny, a little distance below the flower head. Long-stalked leaves also rise separately. Once, vinegar was made from the leaves and used in poultices. Anemone roots consist of a tough, creeping, brown rhizome which grows horizontally just below the soil surface.

Attractive old names for the wood anemone include candlemas-caps, chimney-smock and moon flower; also smell-foxes, smell-smock and granny's nightcap. The plant was at one time made into an ointment for treating inflammation of the eyes and the Romans gathered the flowers for use as a charm against fever.

Some years ago I found the yellow anemone growing wild like the wood anemone, but with bright yellow flowers. I have returned to the spot year after year but have never found it since.

*8 April 1995*

# NATURE ON THE MOVE

As I write this nature note, I am walking through many acres of boulder clay woodland which lie behind our cottage. Today I am on the look-out for little signposts pointing the way to Spring.

Cuckoo pint is unfurling its coils on the woodland floor as dog's mercury comes into flower. There are bluebell shoots everywhere thrusting through the leaf-litter, and celandine leaves, newly-grown, crowding the edges of the pathway.

I pass many scribbly tunnels in the upper surface of bramble leaves. These twisty, white corridors snaking their way through the leaf tissues are the larval homes of Stigmella aurella – the tiniest moth imaginable, exquisitely feathery, and patterned with gold and purple.

I stop to examine little tufts of primrose leaves, newly-born and endearingly crimpled. Ivy leaves sprawl along the ground by the pathway, prettily patterned with filigree veining.

The wood is quiet, its branches bare; and there are honeysuckle trails greenly leafing the tree trunks here and there. White admirals drift through my mind, for wispy strands of honeysuckle are the breeding sites of these elegant woodland butterflies.

Some of the mosses beside the path are very beautiful, particularly thuidium tamariscinum, or feather moss, its springy tufts exquisitely spread like flattened fairy fir trees.

At last I find what I have been searching for on the woodland floor – the handsome spotted leaf-whorl of an early purple orchid. Astonished, I note that lady's smock is already in bud nearby.

Nature is certainly on the move again.

I notice seedlings are stirring on the woodland floor. How amazing it all is, the way every living thing keeps making copies of itself.

A woodcock takes to the air, winging its way adroitly through the trees, while a wren suddenly scolds me with a warning clockwork churr.

As I leave the wood, I turn over several familiar stones under which I sometimes find Limax maximus, a great woodland slug, handsomely spotted, which fully extended can reach a length of eight inches. I replace the stones exactly as I found them, in order to calm the panicking woodlice. My favourite slug, Limax maximus, is not at home today.

*25 February 1993*

Early Purple orchid *Orchis mascula*

# FASCINATION OF FUNGI

THE world of fungi, with its stinkhorns, stars and umbrellas; brackets, fans and antlers; even birds' nests complete with "eggs", is the most confusing world we are ever likely to encounter, also one of a matter of life and death if we have cookery on our minds.

For nearly all of us this strange world passes us by, simply because its astonishing array of life forms is so difficult to identify. Even the word fungi is tricky to handle, so most of the time we do not use it – the accepted pronunciation being "funjy."

An outing with Reg and Lil Evans sheds light in all the fungal darkness, and in no time at all ignorance becomes an educational adventure not to be missed! A few days ago I accompanied Reg and Lil through 93 acres of boulder clay woodland known as Lower Wood, Ashwellthorpe. Right at the start of our fungal foray, Reg discovered on a standing branch of dead hazel, fruiting bodies like little flowers growing in clusters – charming little cups with "scolloped petals" blossoming on the bark. Encoelia furfuracea, as it is called, is only known on about six other sites in Norfolk, so its find is a really exciting "first" for Ashwellthorpe.

Next we examined Phellinus ferruginosus growing on rotten birch, a beautifully tinted fungus like copper-coloured suede; also Stereum hirsutum, a fungus of great charm, tiered all the way up a woody stem like a stick of little fans made of leather. Lil showed me a slime mould called Badhamia utricularis, a fungus on hazel, like tiny bunches of grapes. We stopped to look at King Alfred's cakes growing on ash, the fruit bodies exactly like buns burnt to charcoal.

As we walked on through the wood, Reg pointed out Coriolus versicolor, a wavy-margined fungus, cinnamon-coloured and pale yellow, its velvety interior exquisitely greened with algae; also a jelly fungus, Exidia thuretiana, growing on a rotten tree trunk, its fused clusters just like spawn without tadpoles.

Lil picked up a piece of old wood. It was stained a beautiful peacock green, the tint, in depth, coming from the thread-like roots of the blue-green fungus, Chlorociboria aeruginascens. The most ordinary piece of wood in no time at all becomes a riveting world you never knew was there!

*21 March 1993*

King Alfred's Cakes or
Cramp Ball *Daldinia concentrica*

## SPECTACLE AND SECRETS OF SPRING'S WELCOME HARBINGERS

CATKINS are dangling on the hazels again! When we were children we used to paint pictures of the very first catkins whose discovery we always delighted in. We used to draw silhouettes of them in Indian ink – not only elegant but very beautiful.

Why is it, I wonder, that lambs' tails are so attractive to children, also those elusive inflorescences of tiny crimson stigmas which are so teasingly difficult to find?

Wordsworth wrote with gladness on discovering a shady nook of hazels clustered with nuts …

"A little while I stood," he said, "breathing with such suppression of the heart as joy delights in."

In these leafless days of winter, I, too, feel the joy of William Wordsworth, on finding the first yellow catkins aslant on the hazels in the chilly winds of January. In this infinitely complex world of ours which staggers the mind with its astounding diversity of species, how miraculous it all is the way the cycle of nature never ceases – catkins, snowdrops, primrose time and bluebell time. And so it goes on.

How important it is for us to wonder, and be amazed at creation, which is something I do every day of my life.

Hazels are beautiful not only for their lambs' tails, but also for their pollen grains which are shed in millions, like gold dust. As the grains are released the wind carries them away in yellow clouds. Each catkin, which consists of a string of male flowers, produces about two and a half million grains of pollen. At the base of each stigma – the female inflorescence clustered like tiny red tassels protruding from a bud – there is a chamber holding the egg. The pollen grain develops a microscopic tube which grows down through the stigma to unite with the egg which swells and becomes a hazel nut, usually one of a cluster, in a leafy husk of deeply scalloped bracts.

Hazel catkins are among the first signs of approaching Spring, though in mild weather they will flower early in the New Year.

Some of the catkins here in Ashwellthorpe are still hard and tightly-bunched, while others are gilded with pollen and fully extended.

For several mornings the meadow behind our cottage has been sparkling with frost, the pit frozen over, and bramble leaves encrusted with ice-spicules have been at their most beautiful.

*25 January 1998*

Common hazel *Corylus avellana*

# TASSELLED BEAUTY

*I* was driving along the new A11 between Cringleford and Wymondham a few days ago, when I suddenly noticed thousands of little flowers bordering the highway in a haze of bright yellow.

Astonished by what I had seen – where no stopping is allowed on the carriageway – I returned the next day determined to find out what was growing on this recently constructed verge. After a long walk, with the traffic thundering past me, I eventually reached the "haze of bright yellow," which turned out to be hundreds of coltsfoot plants which must have been "tipped and levelled" by construction workers while landscaping the A11.

The plants were crowded with beautiful fringy faces, turning the sunny verge into a golden treasury of tasselled flowers. Coltsfoot, a member of the daisy family, thrives in disturbed clay soil, and is one of the earliest of our wild plants to flower in Spring. Its many buds open in the sunshine forming beautiful tasselled discs which are slightly fragrant and pollinated by early bees.

The flowerheads have tiny flowers, or florets, growing in the centre like minute yellow crocuses, exquisitely fashioned and well worth a magnifying glass. The stems are also interesting for they are hollow, like little green pipes, and they are clothed with leafy little scales of a reddish hue. What is so striking about the plants is that they are a mass of buds and blossoms and no leaves, the foliage emerging only after the plants have finished flowering.

The leaves, which are felted with cobwebby threads, used to be dried and smoked like tobacco for the relief of asthma. The plant, also made into cough lozenges and cough medicine, became so associated with chest complaints, it acquired the name of coughwort. And even the generic Tussilago, from the plant's scientific name *Tussilago farfara* is taken from the Latin, tussis, meaning a cough.

The plant has a curious habit of drooping its flowerheads as they die, which re-erect a few days later when the fruit is ripe, as beautiful thick silky "dandelion clocks" full of plumed parachutes.

Coltsfoot has other names including bull's-foot, horse-foot and foal's foot, because the leaves were thought to resemble a horseshoe. These tasselled sun-loving flowers of early Spring have the endearing habit of closing up like daisies do at the end of the day, turning their beautiful flat faces into fringy little brushes for the night.

*27 March 1988*

# ALDER CATKINS

*T*HIS morning I went for a walk along the banks of the River Yare, where there were many acres of wet woodland fringed with common alders. The alder trees, bare and brown, were rouged with thousands of red catkins.

Male alder catkins are thicker and far more beautiful than hazel catkins, and over a period of about five months they pass through a number of pretty colour-changes. The catkins are formed during the summer and they spend the winter in hard, tight little bunches, crimson on the side that faces the light and bright green on the side away from the light.

During February and March the catkins flower in long dangling clusters. They are full of texture and smothered with pretty red spots, and they are quickly dredged with pollen. The tiny female catkins, which are crimson and club-shaped, lie immediately behind the male catkins. The fertilised female catkins grow into solid fruits like little green barrels, which ripen into bunches of very hard, dark brown, corky little cones, full of flat winged seeds. The cones stay on the trees throughout the winter, and the new season's catkins prettily flower on the bare brown wings among the previous season's old woody cones.

Alder is very easy to identify, for it is the only British deciduous tree which bears cones. Alder, which is somewhat irregular and rugged in manner, loves growing with its feet in water, and its quiet modest beauty of dark green rounded leaves often overshades the edges of streams and rivers. Because its wood is so hard and durable, it was often used for submerged supports.

Pretty tables used to be made out of the old knotted trunks of alder trees because the wood was so attractive with its varied patterning and reddish-brown hues. The wood was also used for clog-making and shoe soles. And the hard woody little alder cones were once used by fishermen instead of corks to buoy their nets above water.

*9 March 1987*

Alder Catkins *Alnus glutinosa*

# OUT WITH A BAT EXPERT

GOING out with John Goldsmith is always a delight for me, especially when we are on safari looking at bats. For we both think bats are fascinating – which indeed they are.

Harmless and highly protected, misunderstood and even feared, these "furry mice with umbrella-like wings" are severely on the decline. All bats everywhere need our help and encouragement, even affection, not least from those who love our churches.

A few days ago John and I drove to the edge of Breckland, and there, in the middle of a wood, where no-one would suspect it, was an Aladdin's cave, enthrallingly occupied by natural history treasures.

The Aladdin's cave, now a hibernaculum, was once a second world war USAAF bomb group operations' centre, bustling with people in its 26 rooms. Today, doors and windows have been blocked and the building is as dank and empty as a cave.

The first thing John pointed out to me was a bat-brick in which neatly tucked there was a hibernating natterer. Nearby, living in the dark, was a large female cave spider (Meta menardi) – reddish brown and mottled and surprisingly glossy – for which there exist only about five county records.

This handsome, long-legged, large-bodied spider is also a cellar-dweller and of course a cave-dweller. I had never seen so many hibernating herald moths before, their ragged, brown forewings brightly marked with orange. A long-eared hibernating bat, its ears tucked beneath its wings, was hanging on a wall, just beneath a ceiling.

What enthralled me as much as anything was a remarkable carpet of spleenwort growing on the floor of a dimly-lit room – an exquisitely beautiful fern of great delicacy.

Room after room revealed cave spiders living in the dark; herald moths and peacock butterflies asleep on the walls; and yet another delight, a furry Daubenton's bat hibernating behind rotten wood attached to a wall; also a long-eared bat, its little face a portrait, centred and framed in the entrance of a water pipe.

We left this clammy building and locked an impregnable, iron entrance grille.

How many Americans, one wondered, actually know that their secret operations centre is now a winter dormitory for hibernating creatures, where bat droppings are guarded because they are useful indicators of the life above them.

Even the handsome Limax maximus, a great spotted slug reaching a length of eight inches had found its way in to the dormitory.

*26 February 1993*

# VALUABLE IVY

I always feel that ivy is at its most beautiful when its perpetual greenness gives life to a leafless and lonely winter landscape.

Like holly leaves, ivy leaves are dark green on the upper side, and light green on the underside, and their upper surfaces are often prettily marked like fairy crazy-paving, with a fine capillary network of pale green veins.

When the woody stems are laced and plaited round the trunk of a large tree, overlapping leaves can sometimes give a most pleasing vertical tiled effect.

Ivy produces umbels of starry flowers in the autumn when other blossoms are becoming scarce, and these provide the last great nectar feast of the year for many insects including wasps and flies, honey bees and hornets, and late butterflies.

I rarely discourage ivy, for not only are its climbing shoots and drooping sprays beautiful, but its mantling habit provides nesting places, and a wind-proof sleeping place for birds when other trees have long been stripped of their foliage.

During the winter, the purply-capped ivy berries slowly swell and blacken, and when rose hips and hawthorn berries and other wild fruits have all disappeared, the umbels of ivy berries, uninjured by frost, become a feast particularly for blackbirds and thrushes and woodpigeons at the end of winter. Contrary to popular belief, ivy, so often falsely accused, does not live parasitically on trees, as mistletoe does, penetrating its host and absorbing nourishment. Ivy's feeding roots are in the ground and the root-like fringes along the stems are adhesive fibres enabling the ivy to cling to the tree against which it is climbing.

Ivy has long been used for decorating churches, and it was hung up in people's homes in days gone by because it was believed it had protective powers against malicious goblins.

Cups were once carved out of ivy's woody stems, in which drinks were left to stand, because it was believed that the steeped drink was more effective in easing pain. In ancient times ivy was used to decorate the shields of warriors, and to crown the brows of poets.

When Catherine Parr's coffin was opened long ago it was discovered that she had a wreath of ivy entwining her temples.

It is tempting to wonder if any traces of that ivy corondal still exists round the royal withered brow today.

*12 February 1987*

Common Ivy *Hedera helix*

# A SNOWDROP PILGRIMAGE

RECENTLY I went on a very beautiful snowdrop pilgrimage to Walsingham Abbey, which will linger in my mind for many years to come. For in this deeply hallowed place there were many unbroken acres of snowdrops. The Walsingham story is a very strange and riveting legend dating from the "twilight of Saxon England."

In the year 1061 Richeldis de Favarche, a young widow and Lady of the Manor of Walsingham, had a vision in which the Virgin Mary asked her to build a replica of the house in Nazareth where she had been told of Christ's birth by the Angel Gabriel.

So powerful was this revelation and so inspired was Richeldis, she built a wooden copy of the Holy House which was later enclosed in a stone chapel to protect and enshrine it. In August 1961 excavations within the grounds of Walsingham Abbey overwhelmingly confirmed the site of the chapel, and Holy House built by Richeldis in 1061.

Richeldis had a son, Geoffrey, who gave instructions for the foundations of a religious order to take charge of his mother's Holy House. In 1153 the Augustinians were put in charge of the Holy House and built the Priory whose thought provoking and fascinating remains (with later alterations) stand in the grounds of Walsingham Abbey today.

It is interesting that so often snowdrops and monastic sites go together. Were these pure white flowers in fact used on Candlemas Day? Did the monks plant snowdrops specially for Candlemas Day? Confronted with such tantalizing questions one longs for X-ray eyes to see into the past.

I started my snowdrop pilgrimage in the wood beside the drive which was frosted with snowdrops, buttered here and there with aconites. What I found so appealing was the way the River Stiffkey wound its way through the snowdrops – the "snowbells" nodding on their finely arched necks in their thousands in a bluish-green sea of speared leaves.

I left the wood and walked through a little door into the priory precincts where I discovered the most riveting ruins steeped in religious history, with small English yew trees growing high up in the flint work.

Standing there, I was haunted by the silence of a thousand years of passing history, and the enduring remembrance of the soaring triumphal arch of the remains of the east window, a testimony in stone to those long-vanished in the medieval dust.

I noticed a number of wrens flitting about like little brown leaves with wings. I continued on my way round the wood among the snowdrops, returning to the great lawn.

I stood there captivated by the thought of Richeldis and her vision in 1061, and of the little wooden Holy House she had built on "this great lawn," and I longed for those X-ray eyes to see what she looked like, and to see the stream of medieval kings and queens who had worshipped at her shrine. I finished my pilgrimage by climbing through the little door in the gatehouse and out into Walsingham High Street.

High above me in the flint work leaning out of a window was a curious stone carving of a porter "watching" everyone below passing along the street, and particularly those wishing for admission to the gatehouse. I drove home my mind peopled with Richeldis, her son Geoffrey, the Augustinian monks and all the kings and queens and other pilgrims who had worshipped in the little Holy House – a rich and religious pageant, gone for ever.

My last thoughts were of those acres upon acres of snowdrops across the Abbey grounds. Did the monks plant those snowdrops for Candlemas Day celebrations? I wonder.

*18 March 1989*

Snowdrop *Galanthus nivalis*

# THE BRAVE BEETLE

*I* have often wondered how an insect, the devil and a coach and a horse, ever became linked together to form such a nightmarish name for a beetle. Its earliest known occurrence dated 1840 in the Oxford English Dictionary, but I suspect probably lost much further back in the mists of mythology.

A few days ago, Mrs. Doy, of Flordon, and I were examining dead tree stumps in an advanced state of decay along the boundary of Flordon Common.

We were searching for the larvae of the lesser stag beetle and examining gallery patterns and holes bored in the rotting wood, when a large and fast-moving Devil's Coach Horse suddenly appeared from underneath a loose piece of bark.

Few beetles are as sprightly as a Devil's Coach Horse, and we had no specimen box to put it in for further study, so we popped it into a woollen glove where it disappeared along one of the fingers.

The beetle is running about on the floor as I write this nature note, cocking its tail like a scorpion at our dog's investigating nose. It has a lively pair of antennae which it stops to groom with its front legs, and it curves its abdomen underneath itself and grooms the tip with its hind legs.

The beetle is sooty black and slim and it measures 1¼ inches.

Its wing cases are very short and stubby leaving half the beetle with a segmented abdomen which is sinuous and very exposed. Unlike most other beetles whose abdomens are totally covered by their wing cases. When I touch the beetle it responds with instant alarm arching its slender abdomen over its back as menacingly as any scorpion, at the same time opening and closing its pincer-jaws sideways.

Empty threats to me ... but probably not to birds and mammals and small creatures hunting for something to eat, where a threatening posture and defiant attitude might appear formidable.

The Devil's Coach Horse is a carnivore of gardens and woodlands eating many small creatures including smaller beetles, caterpillars and woodlice, spiders and worms, insect larvae and earwigs.

It is also known as the Cocktail beetle, and when the tail is curved over its back it is capable of emitting a repellent vapour in the face of predators.

This brave little "horse" from the Devil's Coach, whose tail was once believed to cast a curse, is daunted by nothing, and it should never be destroyed for it feeds on many of the gardener's enemies.

*28 March 1988*

# PUSSY WILLOWS

SILKY-SOFT, exquisitely tactile and furry, pearly-grey pussy willows have a smooth velvety beauty all of their own. This morning I went to look at a large male goat willow (also known as great sallow, pussy willow, palm, or palm willow) growing in sticky, clayey soil. The twigs were covered with pussy willow catkins, like oval knobs of silky down.

In a week or two the tree will be ablaze with stamens tipped with anthers of ripening pollen. Male goat willow is truly beautiful in spring when its golden diadems of stamens are seen against a cerulean sky. Female goat willows are far less spectacular, with silver-green catkins and arched styles.

Both male and female pussy willow catkins have tiny nectaries visited by bees, and beekeepers in the past planted these trees because pussy willow nectar was taken by the bees to fill honeycombs in Spring, when few other plants were in flower.

Goat willow is so-called because it has a scent which is considered to be like that of goats, and also because goats were fond of eating the catkins. Goat willow wood was used at one time for making handles for agricultural implements, and also for making clothes pegs, teeth for rakes, and axe handles. The bark, like other types of willow, contains salicin, a substance with medicinal properties.

Pussy willow, also known as palm, is carried in place of palms in some parishes on Palm Sunday. It is also used for decorating churches at Easter, both of which suggest that at some time in the past the church must have adopted pussy willow in place of palm fronds – strewn in the path of Christ on his entry into Jerusalem.

Pussy willow, so sweetly named, grows in woods and hedgerows, and alongside water. It is a quietly beautiful tree and its fossil pollen records show that it has thrived in Britain for more than 100,000 years.

*11 March 1987*

Goat willow *Salix caprea*

# BUTTER-YELLOW HERALDS

On March 13 I saw my first brimstone butterfly of the year, a splendid, sulphur-coloured male winging its way across the garden in the sunshine.

Where, I wondered, had it been hibernating? The first brimstone is always an excitement and I rushed to the window to watch this lovely, butter-winged insect on its leisurely flight, till it was out of sight.

We have had brimstone butterflies in Ashwellthorpe for over 30 years, which always surprises me because in all that time I have never yet found its larval food plants – the purging buckthorn and the alder buckthorn – anywhere in the area.

The butterfly, however, is very much a nomad and is known for its appearances a long way from its food plant. The female brimstone, a ghost of its partner, is very pale and milky compared with the butter-coloured brightness of the male.

The butterfly has an astonishingly long life of up to 11 months, in fact the longest of any or our butterflies. The life span of most of our species is two to three weeks, apart from the peacock (10½ months), the comma (8½ months), the small tortoiseshell (10½ months), the large tortoiseshell (9½ months).

These harbingers of spring, sometimes as early as February, and even January if the weather is fine, always concern me with their conspicuous yellow flight which must invite the attention of birds, though I have yet to see a brimstone molested by a bird.

The brimstone butterflies now on the wing emerged from their chrysalises last August, feeding on energy-rich nectar particularly from mauve and purple flowers such as those of the buddleia and purple-loosestrife, thistle crowns and knapweed heads, scabious and teasel, before going into hibernation. The butterfly is also a pollinator of primroses in the Spring.

It is an interesting thought that the brimstone is probably responsible for the contracted word "butterfly," originally a "butter-coloured fly!"

Its wings are veined like a leaf and held in such a way that the insect when hibernating has an indetectable leaf-like camouflage among evergreen leaves. There is even a "spot of imperfection" like iron-mould in the centre of the "leaf!"

A little while ago, I came across a fascinating photograph of a hibernating brimstone hanging downwards among ivy leaves. There was snow on the ivy leaves… and quiet unbelievably… most of the brimstone butterfly was covered with snow too!

*24 March 1993*

# A SPECIAL PLACE FOR MOTHING

ONE of my interests, ever since childhood, has been a passionate enthusiasm for rearing moths, particularly the nobility of the British moth world – the spectacular hawk-moths.

It has therefore been a great pleasure for me over the last year to go "mothing" with Gerry Haggett, an expert on the larvae of British lepidoptera, and Michael Hall, the author of An Atlas of Norfolk Butterflies, in the 93 acres of ancient woodland known as Lower Wood, behind our cottage, which is an SSSI of regional importance being one of the top five woodland sites in Norfolk.

A few days ago I received a list from Michael Hall of the moths recorded in Lower Wood during 1993 – 127 species – the visits taking place during May, June, July and September. Many have beautiful names such as peach blossom whose forewings are patterned with petals, scallop shell and clouded silver; light brocade, dusky brocade and dark brocade; rosy rustic, burnished brass and angle shades.

Others have quaint names such as the snout, the shuttle-shaped dart and the V-pug and the shears. The privet, eyed, poplar and elephant hawk-moth were all recorded in the wood. I was pleased to see the puss moth mentioned – for which I have a great love – and the lobster moth, both of which have the weirdest of caterpillars.

The emeralds, as beautiful and fragile as butterflies, were represented by the large emerald and common emerald. The common lutestring, widely distributed throughout Britain but only sparsely recorded in Norfolk, was also present, as were the seraphim and sloe pug. The sloe pug, Michael Hall tells me, is grossly under-recorded both nationally and in Norfolk.

By far the largest numbers, to date, of the small white wave, associated with ancient woodlands in Norfolk, are to be found in Lower Wood, Ashwellthorpe where I feel a good start has been made. I wonder what we shall find this coming year? There is nothing quite like that sense of expectancy and the excitement of being isolated in a wood in the middle of the night studying moths drawn to mercury vapour lamps having a record of continuous cover, and mentioned in the Domesday Book.

*26 January 1994*

Death's-head Hawkmoth *Acherontia atropos*

# GILDING THE CHURCHYARDS

Winter aconites introduced to Britain 400 years ago, have become widely and beautifully naturalised, gilding the ground in gardens, woodlands and churchyards with their carpets of globe-shaped chalices.

Recently, Gwen Cooper invited me to look at the aconites in Hempnall churchyard, whose medieval church has been so astonishingly and sensitively reorganised to meet the needs of the twentieth century.

These early splashes of gold among the gravestones were beautiful with a vast drift of snowdrops brilliantly buttered with aconites behind the churchyard wall.

On my way home, I called at other churchyards within the Hempnall group ministry. There were sweeping crops of snowdrops in Morningthorpe churchyard and a few golden scatters of aconites among the lichened graves.

Morningthorpe, hidden among winding lanes, has a pervading sense of timelessness unscathed by the twentieth century.

I renewed my delight with Shelton parish church, the sheerest joy to visit for anyone with a love of village churches.

Built of Norfolk red brick, faded and rosy, and dappled with grey brick, it is beautiful in its rural loneliness, particularly when the eye travels along the fenestration of its glassy clerestory.

In the churchyard there were more snowdrops gilded with aconites carpeting the resting places of those long gone.

Along the verge near the church, I stopped to look at winter heliotrope, its heart-shaped leaves spreading along the wayside, its flowers so prettily tasseled and powerfully fragrant.

Fritton churchyard was my final call. Here I found a lych-gate, its seats coated with an emerald layer of algal bloom, and snowdrops with a few sweet violets.

I arrived home with an aconite, a fleeting little keepsake from Morningthorpe churchyard, its starry chalice thick with yellow stamens and honeyed with a strong sweet fragrance.

What is so appealing about aconites is the Midas touch they give winter and their beautiful spreading nature like cloth of spilt gold – their butter-coloured blossoms collared with a ruff, their petal-tubes full of nectar hidden beneath the stamens.

*25 February 1990*

Snowdrop *Galanthus nivalis*
and Winter aconite *Evanthis hyemalis*

# EARLY PRIMROSES

WHEN I was a child, Springtime never passed by without excursions into well-loved woods and fields to pick primroses, violets and cowslips, particularly primroses, which we bunched into charming posies and placed in green honey jars, specially kept for that purpose.

Such sweet communion with wild things when so very young remains affectionately in the memory for ever. Today, while walking in the countryside in fickle and chilly weather, I noticed that primroses were already in flower among newly sprung tufts of endearingly crimpled leaves. For flower-loving minds there is nothing quite like that tiny rapture hidden away in us at the sight of the first pale yellow primrose, for primroses are deeply loved and the most cherished of all our sweet wild spring flowers.

Medieval scholars gave the primrose its name: prima rosa – first rose of the year. For like our beautiful wild roses, they too, have five heart-shaped petals.

Primroses have two different kinds of flowers – pin-eyed and thrum-eyed, which grow on separate plants. In pin-eyed primroses the pistil is long-stalked and shows at the top and the stamens are near the bottom of the tube; in thrum-eyed primroses the pistil is short-stalked and at the bottom of the tube, and the stamens show at the top. The pollen grains of thrum-eyed flowers are large and only fit onto pin-eyed stigmas, and the pollen grains of pin-eyed flowers are smaller and only fit thrum-eyed stigmas, thus effections cross fertilisation by pollinating insects, who are attracted to the primroses and honeyguide lines on the petals indicating the way down to the nectar in the base of the flower tube.

Primrose flowers, also known as Easter roses, were used as a flavouring in 17th century recipes, and what is a little sad to think about today are the vast quantities of primrose flowers once used in the making of country wines.

How sweet is the delicate fresh fragrance of primroses, and what dear little flowers these first pale yellow roses really are, proffered from the ground, among puckered tufts of fresh green crimpled leaves.

*8 March 1987*

Primrose *Primulus vulgaris*

# FLIGHT OF THE 'FAIRY BEES'

RECENTLY I have had the most delightful time in a wood, and around the University of East Anglia, watching primrose sprites, also known as humble bee-flies or bee-flies, and somewhat majestically as Bombylius major.

Their scientific name, Bombylius means "the buzzing one". These beautiful sun-loving insects resemble bumblebees in that their rounded bodies are thickly coated with long, orangey-brown hairs.

The nature of adult primrose sprites is delightful, for these fascinating two-winged aeronauts hover and dart like little humming-birds or humming-bird hawk moths in front of flowers in the spring. Lightly touching down on a petal, and with the utmost delicacy, they insert a long thin tubular tongue, held stiffly out in front of them, into a flower to sip nectar.

Their furriness and fairyness is riveting and anyone who had not noticed them before, would after a few moments begin to wonder exactly what they were looking at. Primrose sprites have six long slender legs, furry bodies of about two thirds of an inch, and long slim delicately-beautiful wings with a scolloped brown margin running along the front edge.

Everything about this little aviator is dainty, and over the last three weeks I have been watching them in the sunshine with the same evolutionary awe that steals over me when watching so many other things. The slightest chill however, even on a sunny day, and the primrose sprites are nowhere to be seen.

Primrose sprites, which are harmless mimics of bumblebees, feed on the nectar of many Spring flowers, including primroses, dandelions, violets and bugle and also in gardens on grape hyacinths, honesty and aubretia.

Watching primrose sprites necessitates staying absolutely still and keeping one's shadow out of the way, for the slightest movement, and these "fairy bees" dart away. When not sipping nectar in the sunshine, they sun themselves on leaf surfaces and on patches of sunny soil.

The larval stage of these furrysprites takes place in the nests of solitary or mining bees, where they feed on the honey and pollen stored by the solitary bee for its own larva, and ultimately, alas, on the bee grub itself.

How fascinating are the tiny inhabitants of our world; and how much one can learn about their ways – simply by teaching oneself through one's own eyes.

*23 April 1990*

# FIRST FINE HAZE OF HAWTHORN

*T*ODAY I have been looking at that first fine haze along the hedgerows – that emerald green of the hawthorns which catches the eye now Spring is here.

How lovely are these twigs with their little knots of newly-born hawthorn leaves after spending the winter destitute of green.

Leaf shoots of hawthorn used to be eaten by country children who called them "bread and cheese." This is not particularly appropriate, however, for the leaves do not taste like bread and cheese.

The other day I came across an old recipe for a savoury pudding using freshly picked leaf shoots of hawthorn. It involved rolling out suet crust, covering the surface with the baby shoots with rashers of bacon cut into strips laid on top. After moistening the edges, the dough was rolled up and steamed in a cloth for at least an hour. It was then cut into slices like a Swiss roll and served with gravy.

I wonder if there is anyone in Norfolk who has ever made bacon and hawthorn suet roll?

Local names for hawthorn, which belongs to the Rosaceae family, are numerous. They include quickthorn, may and whitethorn; also hegpeg, hagthorn and bread-and-cheese tree.

Hawthorns, when not flailed into hedgerow shrubs, grow rather slowly and are long-lived for their size.

They produce very hard wood – perhaps because their growth is slow – which was at one time used for making tool handles and mallets, stakes, walking sticks and wood engravers' blocks.

Hawthorn's spiny tangle of fast-growing twigs has been used as a living barrier for about 2000 years, particularly for enclosing livestock. It has contributed more to the patchwork quilt of our landscape, than any other shrub or tree.

When land was enclosed, mainly between 1650 and 1850, landowners planted countless miles of hawthorn as living fences, naturally barbed, which, enriched the landscape.

Richard Jefferies (1848-1887), naturalist and novelist, wrote in 1884: "Without hedges, England would not be England." I agree with him. His words are certainly food for thought as I write, in 1995.

*23 March 1995*

# SPANGLES OF SPILT GOLD

LESSER Celandines – what delight there is to be found in these starry heralds with their glossy rays like tiny pointed sunbeams spangling in the grass just before the greening of the countryside in Spring.

Year after year I am drawn to the beauty of these little flowers alchemising banks and verges, riversides and woodland, and even a few plants with their glossy blossoms can gild the bottom of a ditch with their eye-catching spangles of spilt gold.

A few days ago I was botanising in some damp woodland among a carpet of moschatels delicately ferning the ground with their low-growing leaves and green flowers, when I came across many celandines glittering among crowded patches of heart-shaped leaves.

Each spangle of starry petals was collared by three green sepals, and the little green fruiting head in the centre of the flowers was thickly fringed with yellow stamens. Lesser celandines, which are native to Britain and pollinated by early bees, belong to the buttercup family which includes wood anemones, marsh marigolds and winter aconites.

In days gone by a peppery juice was extracted from the little tubers among the celandine's fibrous roots in the belief that its use would cure piles which the tubers were thought to resemble. A green ointment was also made for the treatment of piles by boiling chopped celandine leaves in lard.

Many wild plants have a place in folklore, and lesser celandines so butter-coloured and waxy were once used to charm more milk from cows.

Celandine comes from chelidon, the Greek word for a swallow, because celandines flower at the coming of the swallows. The plant is also known by other names, including fogwort and pilewort – wort meaning a root or plant.

The lesser celandine, whose starry disks of burnished gold close at dusk, should not be confused with the greater celandine which is totally unrelated, and whose appearance more nearly resembles that of a poppy whose family it surprisingly belongs to.

It is interesting to note that William Wordsworth not only wrote about "his heart dancing with the daffodils," he also loved lesser celandines and wrote a poem about them too.

*29 March 1988*

# SHAKESPEARE'S FLOWER RETURNS

*H*OW lovely! The cowslips are with us again – *"freckled cowslips"* as Shakespeare called them so enchantingly in Henry V.

What an unforgettable word he chose to describe a cowslip. And with what fairy charm he invests the cowslip in The Tempest – *"In a cowslip's bell I lie"* sings Ariel, that wilful sprite.

Today I have been looking at cowslips in the meadow behind our cottage, and have picked a few of them to write this nature note. Their beautiful heads are shaggy with clusters of egg-yellow flowers, each corolla-tube surrounded with a pale-green calyx, prettily toothed and pleated.

If you look inside the yellow petal-rings, there you will see Shakespeare's freckles, which, are orange, though described by him in Cymbeline as "crimson drops."

These freckles are, honey-guides or sign-posts to the nectar at the base of the petal-tube. Cowslips have a distinctive wild fragrance best described as a sweetly-delicious apricot scent.

Cowslips, like primroses, have two kinds of flowers, thrum-eyed and pin-eyed.

If you look at a head of cowslip flowers you will see at a glance whether they are pin-eyed or thrum-eyed, both kinds of flower never being found on the same plant.

Those with thrum-eyes, or rings of anthers, have a stigma further down the petal-tube. Those with a stigma, or pin-eye at the top, have a ring of anthers lower down the petal-tube.

This clever arrangement ensures cross-fertilisation by long-tongued insects, thrusting down the petal-tubes for nectar.

Cowslip wine used to be made with the egg-yellow petal-rings to which was added sugar and water, yeast and lemon rind.

After stirring the mixture every day for a week, it was put in a barrel with the juice from the lemons, and left to ferment. When "quiet" it was corked down for nine months, then bottled. The devastation which must have been wreaked on cowslip populations would, of course, be unthinkable today.

Cowslips were once widely used in cookery. Izaak Walton (1593-1683) in his fishing classic The Compleat Angler 5th edition, 1676, says that minnows prove excellent when fried with egg yolks and cowslip flowers and a little tansy. How much nicer it all sounds than the pre-packed and pre-frozen fish dishes of today.

*16 April 1995*

Cowslip *Primula veris*

# OPENING EACH-OTHER'S EYES

O N E of the lovely things about the old cottage we live in is that it backs on to a meadow and 93 acres of woodland.

The wood is coming into flower at the moment and there are starry stretches of wood anemones, primroses violets and bluebells, and pathways spangling with celandines.

On a recent excursion round the wood with Reg and Lil, we looked at an intriguing little fungus (Hypoxylon fuscum) resembling lentils. It was raised, black and dotted about on dead sticks of hazel. We also looked at the prettiest mycelia I have ever seen, growing on a damp log, exactly like fox fur among emerald mosses – the ginger filaments, rather like roots, of an ink cap fungus.

Opening each other's eyes is one of the delights of walking round a wood with experts. Lil showed me a slime mould (Trichia floriformis) consisting of hundreds of orange-brown, furry little fungi – something I would never have found for myself.

Reg showed me Taphrina carpini growing on hornbeam exactly like the twiggy witches' brooms which grow so intriguingly on birches.

We passed early purple orchids, their leaf rosettes beautifully spotted with purple, among carpets of celandines spangling in the sunshine. Reg found velvet shank fungi (Flammuline velutipes) on some dead wood, which grows in the winter, even in the frost. Surprisingly it can survive being frozen solid!

He also discovered a fungus new to the wood – Catinella olivacea – growing on damp, dead wood; its form, a deep, olive-green saucer complete with upturned rim.

We looked at pieces of dead wood stained a pretty tint of blue-green inside by the fungus, Chlorociboria aeruginascens. This infected wood was formerly used most attractively in the manufacture of Tunbridge ware, as a veneer.

On our way out of the wood I stopped to look at a fungus with great eye appeal – coriolus versicolour – which grows in densely-frilled layers of velvety fans as though each one was made of leather.

Numerous ladybirds were sunbathing in the wood, all glossy and red, warming themselves on leaf surfaces.

Nearby was a drift of lady's smock, budded and petalled in the most delicate shades of lilac.

*17 April 1995*

*Trametes versicolor*
also known as *Coriolus versicolor*

# *Summer*

*Within the infant rind of this small flower
Poison hath residence and medicine power;
For this being smelt, that part cheers each part;
Being tasted slays all senses with the heart.*

Romeo and Juliet
Act 2nd Scene 3rd.

# LOOKING AT LIFE ALONG A LITTLE LANE

*L*ITTLE lanes. How I love little lanes. Leafy little lanes. Little lanes with no one living in them. Little lanes with grass growing down the middle of them.

There is a lane not far from where I live in which I dearly love to wander. The little lane has no importance and does not go anywhere in particular.

Aspens grow along the lane which I often stop and listen to, for the leaves make such a curious patter as they chatter together in the wind. At the moment they have puss moth eggs on their upper surface and tiny black caterpillars with twin tails.

Dog roses on arching sprays overhang the verges. And there are pure white field roses gilded with stamens flowering in the hedgerows.

Black bryony lives there, threading its leaves through the hedgerows like a vine. Yellowhammers sing in the lane, and turtle doves purr continuously and endearingly.

Sometimes I see a little owl perched on the lane's name-plate. And sometimes I see a barn owl patrolling the headlands of the fields nearby.

Bird's-foot trefoil sprawls along the verges, brightening the edges with its yellow flowers and red-streaked flower buds. Honeysuckle riots in the hedgerows among the dog roses and field roses, and dogwood grows there too.

I often ponder over the dogwood, for our ancestors used its little black berries as a source of lamp oil. How tedious the extraction must have been.

Sometimes, while wandering along the lane, I think – "little lane how I love you, and all the wild things that live in you". I love its peacefulness. Its loneliness. The stillness, and its tranquillity.

I love its field scabious bearing amethyst pincushions of stamens. Jack-go-to-bed-at-noon lives in the lane along with germander speedwell, rough chervil, white campions and meadow vetchling.

Ox-eye daisies drift among the feathery grasses which are spattered with field poppies. On rainy days bumble-bees shelter under the umbrella heads of the hogweed flowers.

The little lane is a contemplative little lane in which to meditate upon the wonder of plant life… the marvel and the miracle of the wild things that live there… the mystery of the existence of life itself …

*20 June 1998*

# MISTS OF MUFFLED BELLS

RECENTLY I went for a walk in a Bluebell Wood where a ground mist of little bells, clustering in their multitudes, stretched far away into the dreamy blue distance.

On close examination, many of the drooping flower spikes fringed with tubular bells were of a variety of lilac tints striped with a beautiful shade of purplish-blue.

The wind was blowing through the bluebells – trembling in their thousands deep in the greenshade of the wood and the sun shone through the leaf canopy forming spotlights in the blue flower mists.

As I walked along a narrow path I came across a leafy patch of greater celandine – an unusual member of the poppy family – bearing many four-petalled flowers and looking so pretty with its buttercup-yellow blossoms among the bluebells.

Everywhere I walked there was a lingering fragrance of hyacinths and everywhere I looked there was a transforming carpet of little blue bells misting into the distance. Red campion and cow parsley were flowering among the bluebells, and here and there, there were white bluebells, instantly pretty and striking, emphasising the charm of the blue ones.

I stopped to look inside the white bluebells and found that their petals and sepals were exactly the same as the blue, the blue bells having mauve stamens and greenish-blue ovaries, and the white bells having white stamens and creamy-white ovaries.

Pignut, whose lumpy brown tubers were mentioned by Caliban in the Tempest, and eaten by the hungry in Shakespeare's day, was flowering among the bluebells like a delicate lacy white trimming, and there were many startlingly bright pink flowers of herb-robert.

As I walked out of the wood I stopped to listen to a wren, this tiny musician sweetly piercing the air with its ear-catching trills.

But my delight in the woodland walk with its marvellous blue ground-mist of muffled bells was not yet over, for along the edge of the wood I discovered a beautiful grassy track of speedwell blossoms of the deepest shade of drifty blue, spangling with a blaze of buttercup chalices.

*7 June 1988*

Bluebell *Endymion non-scriptus*

## ALL QUIET AFTER FROGS' AMOROUS FRENZIES

AT the back of our cottage there is a meadow. At the back of the meadow there is a pit. The pit, like thousands of others in Norfolk, was dug either for marl extraction in the 18th or 19th century to improve the texture of farmland, or for daub and clay for local building materials.

Three years ago the pit was cleaned out with a mechanical digger. It was choked with brambles and contained village rubbish including pram wheels, barbed wire and metal drums.

Today, with the loss of so many farm pits deliberately filled and ploughed out, I was determined to restore the pit for wildlife. The results have been delightful.

Watercress and common water-crowfoot now flourish in the pit. Common figwort, water mint and brooklime have appeared at its edges. This year many frogs have made their way to the pit for spawning purposes. Last year there were only a few.

The shallows round the edge of the pit have "boiled" with their amorous frenzies, several at a time grabbing and gripping one another in a turmoil of frogs almost to the point of exhaustion, with legs sticking out of the water for long periods.

The female frogs were mostly clay-coloured, barred and spotted with black; the males, some of them clay-coloured, some greenish, but many large and nearly black.

I was surprised to see how jewel-like their eyes were for frogs in amplexus (the male gripping the female below her "armpits") peeping through masses of floating spawn had eyes with irises glistening with gold.

All activity has now ceased. The pit is glassy and quiet, as thousands of black eggs in clumps of jelly, like beady sago, develop into tadpoles, strung here and there with double-row necklaces of toad spawn.

It is rather surprising how much the colour of the common frog's skin can vary. In July 1996 Joe Darrell of Tacolneston Hall came to see me with a frog. It was pink!

He had noticed it leaping across a lawn in his garden. It was later released where he found it. No pink frogs have been seen since.

I contacted John Goldsmith at the natural history department at the Castle Museum, Norwich, who told me that he had only seen a photograph of pink frogs, or pink frogs themselves, half a dozen times in the last 20 years.

Like albinos they were genetically fixed, lacking darker pigments in their skin. A few years ago, he told me, pinkish-orange frogs were discovered at Sprowston. They were kept in a bath and produced pinkish-orange tadpoles.

*28 March 1998*

# FOAMING QUEEN OF THE MEADOW

ONE of the loveliest plants to be found at this time of year in meadows, wet woodland, fens and marshes, beside rivers, along ditch banks, even choking the ditches most beautifully, is meadowsweet or Queen of the Meadow.

The plants foam with fragrant little flowers of a rare sweetness. A spiraea of the wild, it is far more beautiful than those known to us through cultivation.

Its charm begins long before its flowers appear, for in early spring its wrinkled green leaves unfold on red stems. The compound leaves, with a silvery-green backing and dark green upper surface, are prettily snipped round their edges.

Between the large leaflets are appealing pairs of tiny leaves, and at the base of the leaf there are sharply serrated stipules. No plant could have more beautifully fashioned foliage.

The tiny cream-coloured flowers, with buds like ivory balls, are massed together in feathery clusters. Individually the flowers are very dainty. Together they foam with pale, gold-tipped stamens.

The fragrant invitation with which the flowers sweeten the air attracts pollen-seeking insects only, for they provide no nectar. The leaves when crushed release a fragrance too, due to the presence of oil of wintergreen. At one time they were put into claret to give it a fine relish.

Meadowsweet in Queen Elizabeth I's day was a favourite strewing herb, both for its leaves and its flowers. It was used freshly cut on the floors of halls and banqueting houses in summer time, the heady sweetness of the flowers and the sharper scent of the leaves masking 16th century smells.

The fragrance, according to John Gerard (1545-1612) barber-surgeon and botanist, also made the heart merry, delighting the senses.

The meadowsweet foaming in a ditch in Ashwellthorpe, whose flowers I stopped to smell yesterday, certainly delighted my senses – over and over again. The name meadowsweet, though echoing the natural beauty of the plant to perfection, is a delightful corruption of an old name medesweete given because the plant was used to flavour mead, the Anglo-Saxon drink made from fermented honey.

*15 June 1998*

Meadowsweet *Filipendula ulmaria*

# A WILDLIFE WALK

Hapton Hall estate is managed with conservation very much in mind alongside farming. It was therefore with great delight that I went there a few days ago for a wildlife walk with Connie Doy.

We set out from the farmyard, passing many scented acres of blossoming field beans beside which germander speedwell was in flower, its little spikes a lovesome spell of blue among the grasses, along with field penny-cress so strikingly seeded with circular winged fruits.

We passed a pillbox crusty with bright orange lichen, where we delighted in dog roses, for there is nothing quite like the deep pink petal cups of the first wild roses.

A male white bryony in flower was scrambling over a hawthorn hedge, held in position by tendrils like long, green springs. We passed hemlock, greater knapweed and fumitory in flower, and a spatter of field poppies, their opening petals like crumpled red tissue.

We noted the strong sweet aroma scenting the air round pineapple weed, the charming little leaves of spotted medick, and also bur chervil in flower.

We finished our walk in newly-planted woodland near Tasburgh marshes which were ablaze with red campion, many of the plants jewelled with deep magenta blossoms of an intensely rich tint – a colour I had never seen before and not at all the usual pink of red campion.

We stared in wonder at the feast of campion, which, as Connie Doy remarked, had so many flowers on the plants, they looked like phlox. The tints in the spectrum of pinks were remarkable, back-crossing and hybridising with white campion probably having caused them; some plants with flowers that were dainty and starry, others with blossoms that were large and phlox-like.

Among the vivid display of campions was a marvellous flowery blueness of common forget-me-nots, a-sprawl with scarlet pimpernel blossoms.

Nearby I stopped to look at common storksbill, a plant that always amazes me with its extraordinary clusters of beak-like fruits, which split into long-tailed corkscrews, each with a burrowing seed attached.

The walk had been delightful and we made a note of many insects along the way, including damselflies of red or blue, and black and red froghoppers, also wall butterflies sweethearting together, holly blues and orange tips, and a beautiful female common blue (brown form) each wing with a vivid orange necklace beaded round its edge.

*21 June 1991*

# EXPLOSION OF COLOUR

*L*IKE Claude Monet, the lover of beauty rejoices in fields stippled with poppies – their folded petals like crumpled red tissue, their opening petals like crushed red silk.

How one mourns for the poppies that blazed in the fields of one's childhood: poppies and corn so inseparably linked together

As I write, some words of a forgotten poet come unbidden into my mind – "'Neath the blue of the sky, in the green of the corn, it is there that the regal red poppies are born" – lines written long ago.

How well I remember the poppies' companions, the corn marigolds, spangling in the fields of my childhood with discs and rays of brilliant yellow-gold – the corn marigold and the field poppy, both of them lovers of newly-cultivated land or disturbed soil.

A few days ago, I went to see Ida Holmes, of Flordon Common, who has a two-acre field ablaze with poppies – like the mottling of an impressionist painting. The sheets of scarlet poppies were gilded throughout with tens of thousands of corn marigolds in a picturesque relationship of startling intensity. The field had been ploughed deeply last year and left unsown, and dormant wild seeds brought up to the surface had caused an explosion of living colour in a wonder of red and gold.

Growing among the poppies and corn marigolds were pineapple weeds with their sweet aroma of pineapples, and wild radish with its curious beaded and jointed seed-pods; also wild miniature snapdragons of rosy-mauve with the quaint name of weasel's snout and field penny-cress with its striking spikes of circular winged fruits – a plant once used as an antidote to poisons.

What was so fascinating about the floral wealth of the field was the sheer multitude of seeds which had been brought to the surface producing a most remarkable alchemy of corn marigolds within the fiery blaze of poppies.

It has been estimated that in Britain there are about a hundred million poppy seeds in every arable acre, and that they can last a hundred years before germinating. What a repository is the safekeeping of the soil!

*20 July 1991*

Red Poppy *Papaveraceae*

# WEBBED FEET IN THE MARKET PLACE

A little sight to see happens in Wymondham almost every day, when two mallard – a duck and a drake – "shop" at two different businesses, which are next to one another in the Market Place.

Quite often when I am in Wymondham in the afternoon I stop and stare at this engaging little scene which takes place outside the hot bread kitchen and the neighbouring fish and chip shop. The ducks call for food at both shops, sometimes twice a day, and bread from the one and chips from the other are obligingly put outside for them.

I was told by one smiling proprietor that if they did not put the food out on the pavement, the ducks followed the customers into the shop. Recently, I watched with hair-raising fascination as the two ducks waddled up Damgate Street, turned right, and then waddled all the way up Market Street in the middle of the road among the traffic.

The drake walked ahead making little calling noises to the duck following behind him, and the traffic stopped or slowed down accordingly. As the ducks approached the Market Place, they turned right, waddled over cobbles and steps, and across a wide pavement, arriving safely at the chip shop and bread shop.

The duck has beautifully mottled brown and fawn feathers, the drake, an iridescent green head and neck, yellow bill, orange legs and feet and curly tail feathers. Wild webbed feet waddling in the middle of Wymondham is a strange sight to see.

On one particular afternoon I watched the ducks call on the shopkeepers for their usual bread and chips, and when they had finished their meal they soon waddled off – the duck behind the drake – back into the middle of Market Street, where they stood for a few moments weighing up the "air-strip" choked with traffic.

Then they took off, both of them together quite suddenly rising steeply above an oncoming lorry. They flew down Market Street between the shops, and above a steam of cars, turned left, and went back home down Damgate Street to the banks of the little River Tiffey, which flows so prettily among the flowery gardens at the edge of the town.

Question – to which I would love to know the answer – just how did two wild ducks who live "out of town", ever discover the benefits of "High Street shopping"?

*20 April 1989*

# GILDING THE GRASSY PLACES

*H*OW beautiful buttercups really are with their waxy chalices of burnished gold.

Common things, like buttercups, can be so beautiful, and are no less beautiful because they are common. Yesterday I went "walking through buttercups". It was the kind of thing one did which lent a magic to those long hours of childhood.

Like daisy-chains, the glow of a buttercup under one's chin remains etched in the memory for ever. The sad thing is that as we grow older we fail to notice the little things, like the realm in the middle of a buttercup; its glazed sheen, its fringy ring of golden stamens, its clustered carpels in a central green globe.

The three commonest buttercups in Britain, which are so much alike and in flower at the moment, are bulbous buttercup, creeping buttercup and meadow buttercup. They gild grassy places, often together, and scattered in thousands they turned the meadows and pastures of childhood yellow.

All three kinds of buttercups are visited by bees which take their pollen and nectar. Bulbous buttercups, which are the first of the three to flower, are very easy to identify for the sepals underneath the petal cup are turned back. The plant has a bulbous corm just below the surface of the ground which at one time gave it the curious name of St Anthony's turnip.

Creeping buttercup has upright spreading sepals and furrowed flower-stalks, with creeping runners which root new plants at intervals.

Meadow buttercup also has upright spreading sepals, but has smooth, unfurrowed flower-stalks. It does not have a corm or runners. With a little care it is not difficult to identify the three species accurately.

Buttercups were once used as medicines, particularly extracts of meadow and bulbous buttercups, which were applied to the skin to produce blisters to draw poisons in the body to the surface. This was particularly so with bubonic plague.

Beggars were at one time also known to use buttercups to induce blisters on their skin in order to inspire sympathy. There are many forgotten names for buttercups, including gold cups, gold balls, butter-flowers and butter-churn, also gilted cup and frogwort.

*20 June 1991*

Buttercup *Ranuneulus acris*

# MAJESTIC ARCHITECTURE

SOMEONE said to me the other day: "You must come and lie down and look up at the beautiful canopy of our horse chestnut tree."

Having lain on my back on a bench in the Vatican examining the ceiling of the Sistine Chapel some years ago, I knew exactly what was meant about that vantage-point for examining the canopy of a tree.

It is very rarely, if ever, that we lie down on our back to scrutinise the detailed structure of a massive and majestic tree; and the hidden architecture high up in the dome of the horse chestnut was overwhelming and beautiful from a reclining point of view.

Its fan-vaulting of limbs and branches soared upwards and outwards supporting a dense canopy of foliage, with many of the smaller branches curving downwards and outwards, with sweeping spreads of twigs and leaves.

The sky above was cerulean, and it showed through the leaf canopy in little bits of cloudless blue; and the foliage ranged through a marvellous colour spectrum of lime greens in the sunlight, of leaf greens and shady greens against the blue.

I spent a long time examining the canopy of this tree with its towering mass of foliage composed entirely of large splays of finger-leaflets.

As I looked high into the dome, spotlights of sunshine were shafting through the leaf canopy, and I could see a spotted flycatcher darting from a branch snapping up flying insects.

I finished my examination of this massive tree exactly in the way the owner had suggested, and I decided that its ceiling of leaves with tiny breaks of blue was just as beautiful in its own way, as the ceiling of the Sistine Chapel had been when I studied it some years ago.

I measured the girth of the tree trunk which was exactly ten feet, and I thought with Shakespeare somewhat in mind... "what a piece of work is a tree".

*14 July 1988*

# WONDER OF WHITE

I have been roaming through a sunlit filigree flower-mist of cow parsley with a driftiness and a dreaminess that was exquisitely fragile and graceful.

Trailing through feathery leaves surmounted by myriads of tiny white flowers frothing on dainty umbels spoked with a delicate radial symmetry, is elemental and therapeutic, for there is a healing balm from beautiful things, and ecological harmony the world has forgotten about.

Cow parsley lacily casting its spell along roadsides, untouched by the horrors of overzealous verge-cutting, gives a tracery of unsurpassable bridal beauty. One reader who recently wrote to me about the lanes round his home at Pockthorpe, said that they were "a wonder of white, everywhere."

The wilder the verges, the lovelier they look. For cow parsley mists with their gentle grace have a special aura that is almost indefinable – a floral charisma magically transforming the wayside.

It is sad how we all see flowers so often but do not look at them; do not live with them, even for a few moments – browsing in their busy world of stamens and stigmas; do not learn to love them – which so heightens the levels of one's awareness. Their beautiful colours. The shape of their petals. The architecture of their leaves. Their wild fragrance.

For common plants can be so beautiful. Even their seeds – such well designed investments – with a future locked up so safely inside each one of them. Wild flowers of the wayside – and particularly cow parsley with its compelling fascination – are evolutionary treasures in a world that passes them by, or so often minces them to smithereens with cutters.

We do not explore our wild flowers, or what is left of them, nearly enough. How often while botanising I am overcome with a pervasive and terrible sense of desperation at the way we treat this world. The only earth we have.

Jeremy Bentham (1748-1832) said: "Stretching his hand to catch the stars, man forgets the flowers at his feet." The world is finished as we once knew it – someone said to me the other day. I knew what he meant. For man and Eden have become dangerously out of balance.

*1 June 1987*

Cow Parsley *Anthriscus sylvestris*

# ENCHANTMENT IN THE DARK

As I write this nature note it is nearly two o'clock in the morning and I have just arrived home after spending a magical hour with a farmer and his wife, listening to a nightingale pouring out its song from a tree in the yard of a dairy farm in Fundenhall.

How can one describe the sheer beauty of an hour of matchless music from a little brown bird that has come here to breed from tropical West Africa.

A nightingale singing solo in the silence of the night, with ever-changing strains of liquid notes, is surely one of the most beautiful of all songsters anywhere on earth. Nightingales sing during the day, but why do they sing at night when they can set up a territory in the daytime?

I stood there spellbound and motionless in the darkness of the farmyard – this little brown bird only a few feet away. The buildings on the farm and its tall trees stood all around me silhouetted against the night-sky – its inter-stellar blackness lightened by the radiance of a melon-coloured moon.

Nightingales are more often heard than ever seen, and one is lucky to get even a glimpse of this shy little bird which is bigger than a robin and smaller than a song thrush, and always hidden away in woods and thickets or dense cover.

I left the musician in the tree pouring out its soul in mellifluous strains and walked through the farmyard and passed its buildings, where row upon row of Friesians lay chewing the cud in straw-lined cubicles.

The smell of cows in the coolness of the night was wonderfully warm and farmy. I passed through the farm gates with a feeling of exhilaration – the nightingale behind me, with a song of such matchless versatility, still spilling its liquid notes into the darkness of the night.

*6 May 1988*

# PRETTY WOODLAND FLOWERS

TREES provide shade and shelter, and by their strength and character, beauty and stillness, make woodland "a marvel for the human mind to walk in".

Recently I visited an old oak wood at Thursford. The wood was densely carpeted with bluebells and patched with wood-sorrel whose nodding little white blossoms were prettily veined with lilac.

I doubt whether any other native plant produces leaves like wood-sorrel which close for the night like crowds of little green drop-leaf tables. As early as the 14th-century the leaves were used to flavour salads, their taste when chewed is exactly like lemon juice.

After sampling a few leaves of wood-sorrel, I stopped to finger some trailing ground-ivy, its leaves minty and aromatic and purpled with little flower-whorls.

The mighty oak, a peculiarly British tree, was once called "the father of ships".

I have rarely seen such venerable oaks as those in Thursford Wood, rugged and riven, crooked and geriatric, more picturesque in their old age than ever in their youth, patriarchs still alive in the 20th-century whose lives began in Plantagenet acorns.

At the far end of the wood, which slopes downwards to the upper reaches of the River Stiffkey, I came across a marsh.

The ground was lushly colonised with kingcups and opposite-leaved golden saxifrage in pretty shades of lime green, its glistening carpets of little flowers speckled with gold from yellow-anthered stamens.

Bird cherry was in flower in the wood, eye-catchingly pretty and white, its long racemes of dainty blossoms so heavily fragrant.

I passed many more oaks, some of them pollarded, some awe-inspiringly ancient, and others fantastically shaped.

The last wild flowers I stopped to examine were moschatels, dainty little plants that need searching for, and are easily passed over.

Each cubed flowerhead bore five green flowers, four facing outwards like a town-hall clock, with one on the top facing upwards.

This old oak wood was a sheer delight with its pollarded monarchs and bluebell carpet. Gnarled oak trees deformed with antiquity, have so much strength and character, and all so miraculously unfolded – from an embryonic acorn.

*24 May 1990*

# DANDELION GOLD

DANDELION gold has been dazzlingly bright this year, the gleaming faces of the flowers spangling along the verges like big flat shaggy suns. Contrary to that which is held by most people … I have a high opinion of dandelions! The American poet Lowell said of dandelions – "Dear common flower that growest beside the way, fringing the dusty road with harmless gold …".

The flowerhead of the dandelion is not one flower, but many little florets, all grouped together in a community and functioning as one flower.

If one removes one of the bright yellow flowers from a dandelion's head one can see that it consists mainly of a single, five-toothed petal which is strap-shaped, having five petals in a ray or strap fused together side by side.

At the base of the dandelion's head, which is attached to a hollow stem, there are rings of long green bracts. Some of them stand upright as a guard round the florets, others, often prettily tinged with pink, turn downwards most attractively just like a little collar. In fact the care that has gone into making a dandelion from its sunlike head to its diaphanous clock is awesome.

The transformation of a dandelion's shaggy golden head into a gossamer ball of aeronauts is one of nature's architectural marvels for seed dispersal.

For these travellers in the wind are set free on their journey of life, when the wind gives the signal, suspended by nothing more than the flimsiest of parachutes composed of a ring of hairs. The dandelion's seeds are well worth a few moments' perusal under magnification, for they are pointed to push gradually into the ground aided by minute barbs around the top of the seed to "firm it in".

Sometimes, perhaps while walking along a verge, I think how sad it is to see the dandelion's receptacle left behind – its gossamer ball gone.

For the tonsured head of the dandelion stands tall, white and bare and pock-marked among the grasses, its withered bracts, all turned down, its little life over, but with a genetic stake… a new generation… blown into the future!

*17 May 1994*

Dandelion *Taraxacum officinale*

# PERFECTION OF A HIDDEN NEST

CHRISTINE Brigham of Fundenhall came to see me a few days ago… carrying a flowerpot. She had turned out a courgette which was root-bound and put it in a bigger pot.

While removing the courgette from its original pot, she had discovered to her astonishment two rows of nest cells made from rose leaves, looking rather like cigar butts, running round the inside of the flowerpot.

She arrived at our cottage puzzled by her find, the nest cells in a pile in the bottom of the pot. "Ah, you've had a visitor," I told her. "A leaf-cutter bee has been at work in your flowerpot!" Leaf-cutter bees are a fascination to watch as they cut oval and circular sections from rose leaves, both wild and cultivated. A few years ago I spent a riveting hour or so, watching the arrivals and departures of a leaf-cutter bee at the entrance to a burrow in a flowerpot.

The bee, many times over, flew to the flowerpot with an oval section cut from a rose leaf neatly rolled between its legs, and with a little manoeuvring, disappeared with the leaf section down the burrow in the earth in the flowerpot.

Leaf-cutter bees are solitary bees and there are 227 species of solitary bees in Britain compared with only one species of honey bee. It is the female leaf-cutter bee which, in June and July, builds the cylindrical "cigar butt" cells found in flowerpots and other secluded places.

The flowerpot of nest cells brought to me be Mrs Brigham was intriguing to examine.

The leaf-cutter bee with her powerful, shearing jaws had cut about 100 sections from dog rose leaves. I took a nest cell to pieces. It had been laboriously and beautifully constructed from 10 sections of living rose leaf. And the cell had been provisioned with a sticky mass of honey and pollen.

Somewhere in the cell, though I could not find it even with a magnifying glass, a single egg had been deposited by the bee. What I find so truly remarkable is, that after constructing the sides of the nest cell, the leaf-cutter bee then seals the entrance to the cell with a leaf section cut in a perfect circle!

What is "ordinary" to the leaf-cutter bee seems quite extraordinary to me. Just how have leaf-cutter bees evolved with their truly amazing nest cells – oval sections for the walls, circular ends, each nest cell fitted perfectly into the one behind it, and in this instance all of them down a dark burrow in a flowerpot. Nature's mysteries are remarkable. Needless to say, I re-built the string of nest cells in the original clay flowerpot and filled it with friable earth. A minor catastrophe brought about by re-potting a courgette has been averted!

*14 July 1994*

# ROSES

*I*N an outlying part of the parish of Bunwell, I stopped to explore a high, uncut hedgerow in a riot of neglected beauty – creamy with big flat heads of elder flowers, and sprawling with arching sprays of wild roses pinkly cascading down the side of the hedgerow into a lacy ground-mist of rough chervil.

Why, like so many others before me, do I love the wild rose of England in the way that I do?

Perhaps it is because the moving, magical beauty of their pink petal-cups is so scenic and compelling, especially when seen gracing a hedgerow against a blue sky.

The dog rose, the one I love most of all our beautiful wild roses, produces little groups of deep pink flower-buds enfolded with tufts of endearingly fringed green sepals. The buds unfurl into thinly curved, spherical petal-cups with a fragrance that is sweet and delicate. Each petal is heart-shaped, and five chilly-pink petal-hearts make one wild rose. If you look into a newly opened dog rose, you will find its centre thickly fringed with egg-yellow stamens which are visited by insects for pollen.

Another wild rose love of mine is the sweet briar with deep pink roses among leaflets whose

Dog rose *Rosa canina*

the dog rose, or canker rose with its trailing briars in particular.

Dog roses sometimes have crimson and green mossy balls on their twigs known as "Robin's pincushions" or moss galls. These exceptionally beautiful galls are the enchanting grouped homes of the larvae of a tiny gall-wasp. The countryman's name "Robin's pincushions" is a very old one, and refers to the woodland sprite Robin Goodfellow.

As well as the dog rose, sweet briar, field rose and burnet rose there are other wild roses growing in Norfolk which I would dearly love to see, such as the small or lesser sweet briar and the downy rose – a shrub whose arching stems with downy leaves bear pink or white roses.

To me, there can never be anything more lovely than an arching spray of wild pink roses wandering astray in a hedgerow, and no garden rose can ever equal the simplicity and beauty of this wandering wildling rose that is forever England.

glands produce and aromatic oil smelling of fresh green apples, which is particularly noticeable after rain has fallen.

Field roses which grow in hedgerows in Ashwellthorpe, Bunwell and Wattlefield, are white with many yellow stamens. They have rounded, neatly sepalled rose-buds with none of the the tufts of the dog rose.

Recently, while walking near the coast I came across the burnet rose whose growth habit is so different from other wild roses. The rose was low and shrubby, with fiercely-armed stems densely spined with prickles and bristles. The rose-buds were charming and almost stripy as the green sepals parted revealing the white petals. The opened rose, which had such a sweet scent, was filled with a thick array of yellow-tipped stamens, each white petal slightly notched with a touch of lemon at its base.

Shakespeare mentions roses in his works more frequently than any other flower. Some of his most exquisite poetry was inspired by them,

Left: Field Rose *Rosa arvensis*
Right: Sweet briar *Rosa rubiginosa*

# NIGHT AIR IS FILLED WITH A SWEET SMELL

THE scent of honeysuckle in the hedgerows at the moment is seductively sweet in the evenings. No wonder the 17th-century diarist Samuel Pepys called honeysuckle "the trumpet flower whose bugles blow scent instead of sound". Nothing could be more enchantingly written.

John Parkinson, botanist to Charles I, writing in 1629, said: "The honeysuckle that groweth wilde in every hedge, although it be very sweete, yet do I not bring into my garden, but let it rest in its owne place, to serve the senses of those that travel by it."

Today, how few, if any, write so appreciatively of our wild plants.

This world is very old. How did honeysuckle, a fanfare of trumpets, so sweetly scented and so rich in nectar, ever evolve down those awesome vistas of time?

Honeysuckle, or woodbine, is the loveliest of our wild climbers and twiners, coiling clockwise round other shrubs in a hedgerow sometimes so tightly it can deform the trunk of a young tree into a barley sugar twist.

In fact a highly-prized find used to be a blackthorn stem distorted by honeysuckle into a corkscrew because it made such an attractive walking stick.

Today I picked a few stems of honeysuckle before flail-cutters trim a roadside hedge (what a crime to flail such a plant).

The subtle colourings of the honeysuckle were beautiful. The outer ring of trumpets in the flower clusters were shades of champagne-gold. The inner flowers, unopened, were flushed with dusky-red and tinted at their tips with crimson. The stamens flared from the open mouths of the flowers, each with an anther like a tilting see-saw at its tip.

Honeysuckle is primarily a flower of the night, diffusing a powerful incense into the air after dusk. The realm of a cluster of honeysuckle flowers is enchanting, the incense exceptionally sweet.

Pollinating hawk-moths, such as the elephant hawk-moth and the privet hawk-moth, must find the fragrant appeal of honeysuckle compelling, as they probe deeply with their long tongues down the long corollas, searching for the sweet nectar.

*18 June 1998*

Common Honeysuckle *Lonicera periclymenum*

# RAUCOUS MUSIC OF ROOKS

IT all started a few Sundays ago. I was attending Morning Prayer at Bracon Ash Church.

Outside, it was one of those marvellous English days, the churchyard strewn with violets and primroses. Everything was green and growing and the sun was actually shining.

For a few precarious moments I felt drawn to those famous words of Robert Browning's – "God's in his heaven – All's right with the world!" In the background, rooks were cawing – the whole service was accompanied by the wild calls from the rookery.

For a fleeting moment I thought, how English England still really is, in some of its rural corners. Coming out of church I stopped to examine the rookery in Church Wood nearby, and the more I examined it the more involved my interest became, so much so, that I returned later in the day with my binoculars and a tape recorder.

I recorded the raucous music of rooks' voices as they called and answered one another all over the rookery – a dissonant, harsh-toned chatter of "chacking" and cawing.

The rooks' nests were amazing when examined through my binoculars. They were very unruly and like a pile of kindling perched among twigs and branches. The trees in the wood which had twiggy crowns were more favoured than others, one tree in particular having 26 nests in it, some very close to one another, other trees having one or two. Just before evening, rooks came in from the arable fields nearby, blackening tree-tops in the rookery, and all perching in the same direction.

For no apparent reason, they would all suddenly rise from their roosting places in a cackle of cawing, and, manoeuvring simultaneously, they would swirl round the top of the rookery.

There was a great deal of settling down for the night, then unsettling and swirling round the rookery again. I decided there and then that I liked rookeries. They made the wood lived in. Really lived in. Particularly with their restlessness and the tumult of their voices.

I returned to the wood at midnight to study the rookery under the cover of darkness. The wind was soughing through the wood, the sky twinkling with stars through the twigs of the rookery. I was surprised to find, the chatter of rooks voices "still going on", but muted, and with the volume of the rookery "turned down", as here and there in the rookery they softly cawed and chattered to themselves, and to one another.

Just why do rooks nest communally in rookeries like housing estates in tree-tops? And why do they nest so high up in the slender upper branches when there are more stable ones lower down?

*23 April 1994*

# HORSEY MERE

$\mathcal{R}$ECENTLY I have been revelling in the beauty of Horsey Mere – its reedy landscape, its subdued colours, its watery solitude and its picturesque wind pump built to drain the marshes. Here, in this sanctuary for wildlife as well as for the human spirit, I went for a walk which filled me with delight at every turn.

Along a twisting overgrown path edged with creamy-white climbing fumitory, I passed purple-spotted stems of hemlock, shoulder-high with fairy umbels and feathery leaves, and here and there I noticed belladonna with muted mauve thimble-bells.

There were many flat creamy heads of elder flowers and prickly thickets of wild roses. I stopped to stare at the last of the wild roses – for what ecstasy there is in the presence of a wild rose. Further along the path I passed tall clumps of hemp agrimony with tightly-budded pink heads, and hedge woundwort with its beautifully soft felty leaves and deep magenta flowers, much visited by bumblebees.

I stood very still for a few moments with my eyes closed, listening to all the sounds around me – the busy hum of insects, the scratchy chatter of warblers, and the wind hissing through the reeds. I walked on, passing patches of delicate pink valerian and tall magenta foxglove spikes, tumbling with leopard-spotted finger-bells – the most beautiful of all honey-guides for bumblebees.

As I walked further into this blessed wilderness I passed a group of white foxgloves with speckled and spotted throats, and I opened one of the finger-bells to examine the hidden purple artistry of its beauty from within.

I met tansy time and again along the pathway, and I picked one of its prettily-cut leaves which I bruised between my fingers, breathing in slowly its aromatic smell. Near the end of my walk I came across beautiful spikey magenta fires of rosebay willow-herb, and eye-catching scrambles of tufted vetch, all purply-blue and busy with bumblebees.

I finished my walk with the thought that here at Horsey Mere was everything I hold most dear... wilderness... solitude and tranquillity, and a loneliness... that had not been ruined.

*31 July 1987*

Rosebay willowherb *Chamaenerion augustifolium*

# AN AMAZING LIFE STORY

*I*VY-LEAFED toadflax which sprawls so prettily from crevices in walls, particularly old walls, is in flower at the moment.

A plant of gracefulness, trailing stems and dainty charm, it is also known as mother of thousands, the name by which I knew it as a child, alluding no doubt to its picturesque succession of little flowers. The fact that the plant flourishes in walls where the living to be had from cracks and crannies must be somewhat precarious, almost ascetic at times, is a wonder all on its own.

As I write, I have a few trailing stems of ivy-leafed toadflax beside me. Its little leaves, at intervals along the stems, are charmingly ivy-shaped. The flower buds at the base of the leaf-stalks are purple, the flowers themselves, mauve. Each flower looks like a baby snapdragon but with a purplish-mauve spur at its rear.

Tiny as it is, the flower is exquisitely provided with honey-guides, for pollinating bees in the form of purple streaks on the upper lip and inviting yellow mounds at its mouth. If you pinch the flower to open it, down the throat you can see orange-coloured hairs, above which there are four stamens bearing white pollen. Nectar trickles between the stamens into the spur from which it is collected by visiting bees.

A most remarkable thing happens to ivy-leafed toadflax as its seed capsules form and ripen, which I should think is almost without parallel. The plant's stalks, previously holding the flowers facing away from the wall and projecting through the foliage, actually curve round towards the wall until the capsules, quite incredibly, are firmly pushed into cracks and crevices.

In 1850 a deputation went to see the Chancellor of the Exchequer concerning the abolition of the iniquitous Window Tax. To illustrate that the blocking out of light directly affected one's health, they produced an ivy-leafed toadflax, a flourishing part of which had grown with full access to light, and a light-starved part which had been accidentally cut off from the light and was weak, small, flowerless and fruitless. The argument was so telling, as it illustrated the depressing effects of darkened dwellings, that the Window Tax resistors gained their point!

*19 May 1994*

Ivy-leaved Toadflax *Cymbalaria muralis*

# THE CALL OF THE WILD

THE call of the wild draws me like a magnet to the sheer green magic of Upton Fen.

Thank God for wetland wilderness among the arable fields of Norfolk, wilderness away from this world where the mind, to quote Andrew Marvell (1621-1678) can "withdraw into its happiness".

Upton Fen, a spring-fed Site of Special Scientific Interest west of South Walsham village, covers 130 acres of fen, dykes and alder carr, young oak woodland, sedge and reed beds.

In the early years of this century the fen produced crops of gladden, or fen-hay, used for horse bedding.

On a recent pilgrimage round the fen I stopped with interest to look at a charming little scene of bright blue damselflies flitting about above water soldiers, spiky-starred in a turf pond.

I passed through soaring woodland jungly with honeysuckles trailing from on high. Little blue skullcap was in flower deep among the damp grasses, and pretty green marsh ferns fringed the footway, close to my feet.

I stopped to look at marsh pennywort in quaint little carpets of penny-shaped leaves, also at valerian and seflheal, and to breathe in deeply the rare heady sweetness of the foaming flowers of the meadowsweet.

I continued with my visit along "fox-dropping walk", as I always call it, looking at marsh bird's-foot-trefoil, cyperus sedge, so beautiful and green, and bright yellow water-lilies with brandy-bottle seed capsules floating in a dyke.

Here I stood for a few moments listening to "The Spirit of Norfolk", the wind in the reeds, hissing so lightly with a fine dry rustle.

Suddenly I "ran out of reeds" that had been towering above me and arrived at a vast, atmospheric view of grazing marshes with little white sails passing through the landscape in the the distance. Windmills, their use introduced from Holland in the 17th-century to drain land and pump the water into dykes and rivers, could be pinpointed in the far distance.

This serene and expansive view of grazing marshes, windmills, sailing boats, churches and cattle under a vast open sky is the quintessential landscape of Norfolk.

As I said at the beginning of this note, the call of the wild draws me like a magnet to the sheer green magic of Upton Fen... with this truly remarkable viewpoint of Norfolk.

*17 July 1992*

# FOXGLOVE'S MAGIC

*F*OXGLOVES – so bold and bright and beautiful – are perhaps the most striking and stately of all our wild plants.

Their handsome blossoms hang in ever lessening bells towards the tip of the spire and have twisted flower stalks so that "falls" of magenta spotted finger-bells hang to one side.

The hidden beauty within the foxglove's flower-bell is something I have long delighted in, for they are richly spotted and speckled with deep purple honey-guides.

During the last few weeks I have looked inside innumerable foxglove bells and "the bee's eye view" is magnetically pretty.

Over the last month I have been watching a group of 40 wild foxgloves, and one of the most fascinating things I noted was that they were perpetually besieged by bumblebees, who climb up and reverse down each flower-bell in silence, and then, loudly hum along to the next bell where they forage for nectar. The spotted mouths of the flower-bells are whiskery within, the silken white hairs preventing any shed pollen from falling out, and small nectar-stealers from creeping in.

A week ago I ran a number of bumblebee tests on their visiting times to the finger-bells. I was very surprised to discover that the last bumblebee left the foxgloves at 9.45pm and the first one actually "started work" at 3.30am!

There is a pretty little moth mottled in brown and orange called the foxglove pug, whose green caterpillar lives inside the foxglove's bell sewing the edges of the flower together with silken threads to form a retreat. Inside it feeds on the stamens and the unripe seeds.

However picturesque the name may be, it is not thought that foxgloves were ever gloves for foxes, the word glove probably having been derived from the Anglo-Saxon "gliew" – a musical instrument with many small bells, and fox from "folk's", meaning little folk or fairies.

The foxglove, a poisonous plant, has given medicine the powerful drug digitalin which is used in small doses in the treatment of heart disease. Country medical practitioners used to dry the leaves and prepare extracts which were so highly valued that in Paris this handsome plant was often painted on the door-posts of apothecarys' dwellings.

*14 July 1990*

Foxglove *Digitalis purpurea*

## WHO WILL LISTEN TO THE HEDGEROW'S LAMENT?

*I* am a hedgerow! Let me begin my story by saying life is very hazardous. Destiny is my problem. Will I be butchered by flail cutters, or trimmed neatly? Will I be grubbed out? It is just possible I suppose that I may be allowed to remain where I am for years to come. If only I could do what I like sometimes, instead of growing as I am told to grow.

As a hedgerow deep in the countryside I often wonder about my origins. I must have been of importance at some time. Who planted me, for instance? And why did they plant me at all? For I know as a structure I am man-made.

Perhaps I once formed part of the boundary of an Anglo-Saxon settlement. Or maybe I am a woodland relict left when fields were cleared on either side; or an Enclosure hedge passed by Act of Parliament to end the open field system. Or perhaps I was deliberately planted as a stockproof hedge.

The real problem is that I am not sure of my status any more. It seems to have gone. I feel a nuisance. A burden. A financial liability as there is no real need for me as a proprietary boundary or stockproof barrier any more.

What about a corridor for wildlife? Isn't that important? Don't hedgerows as sanctuary strips make wildlife richer? There are times during the year when I really do feel rather beautiful. Doing my bit for the countryside.

In spring I am snowy with blackthorn. In May it is hawthorn blossom. I know I am useful in that I provide support for many climbers, including honeysuckle, dog roses and field roses. The arching sprays of the dog rose fill me with pride. The fanfares of honeysuckle trumpets sweeten the air with their incense. Black bryony berries adorn me like coloured beads threaded on a vine. Traveller's-joy and bellbine need my support too. One thing I do know. I can be of great scenic value to the countryside.

Yesterday was extremely unpleasant for me. A tractor flail tidied up nature. It stripped me of my beauty. I was ruthlessly defoliated… an unsightly mess of torn branches with frayed ends. I know my wounds will heal, and that I shall produce green shoots again. But at what a cost. I have lost my hedgerow harvest for winter bird food through the ugly management of the mechanised trimming.

I feel the saddest of sights. I am now less than two feet from the ground. Stripped of my functions. I am of no landscape or wildlife value any more. Tell me – do I really have to be such an ecological disaster in the interests of economy?

Richard Jefferies said in 1884: "Without hedges, England would not be England." I wonder what he would say about me!

*15 August 1998*

# ORANGE-TIP A LATE SPRING BEAUTY

OVER the last week or so I have been watching the erratically-pretty flight of the male orange-tip, a colourful late spring butterfly with unmistakable wingtips. It is only the male butterfly that has these lovely orange wingtips, the female being white with black wingtips.

The female is easily dismissed as a small white – that is, until you notice the undersides of the hind wings which are a pretty patchwork of mossy-green and white. This dappled coloration, which is also on the hind-wings of the male orange-tip, provides a perfect camouflage when the butterfly is at rest.

These attractive insects, of which there is only one generation a year, live for about 18 days, though probably less than that for many of them. Thirty-three different kinds of plants in the Cruciferae family have been recorded bearing the eggs of the orange-tip. By far the commonest is the lilac lady's smock of damp grassy places, and the garlic mustard of the wayside, better known as Jack-by-the-hedge.

Each female only lays one egg on its chosen plant, positioning it on the stalk of a flower which will have become a seedpod by the time the caterpillar hatches a week later. The egg, which is spindle-shaped with about 18 keels and many ribs, changes colour from greenish-white to yellow, then orange, and before hatching, to pale brown.

The tiny caterpillar, pale orange on hatching, eats its own eggshell and any other egg of its own species it encounters, for the orange-tip is a cannibal. If another female orange-tip lays an egg on a plant already occupied – the older caterpillar will eat the younger one. The caterpillar grows to its full size in about 26 days feeding mainly on a rich diet of ripening seedpods, though it will eat buds, flowers and leaves. It is bluish-green and hardly distinguishable from the seedpod on which it feeds.

The caterpillar pupates in a triangular chrysalis, normally pale brown, sometimes clear green, for about 11 months. The mossy-green and white patterning on the under-side of the orange-tip's hindwing is in fact an optical illusion. For not one of the scales is actually green! This curious cryptic effect is brought about by a mixture of black and yellow scales.

In 1748 the orange-tip was recorded as the wood lady or the Prince's Orange. By 1775 it had been changed to lady of the woods, and by 1795 to orange-tip.

What we see as the charm or beauty of the male orange-tip butterfly is really a warning coloration, for this species is one of the most unpalatable of all British butterflies.

*16 May 1995*

# THIS OTHER EDEN

$\mathcal{A}$S I write this nature note, I have just returned from a rainy ramble through a spring-fed bog on Flordon Common, one of the best remaining calcareous spring-fed fens in Norfolk.

On our way across the common towards the bog, we passed blue spires of bugle soaring among thousands of waxy buttercups gilding the grasses with their chalices. The fragrance of young water mint, once used for smelling salts, scented our way here and there bruised by our passing feet.

Ragged-robin was in flower, so strandy with the raggedness of its eye-catching charm. Yellow-rattle, and its blossoms being visited by pollinating bumble-bees. We stopped to look at germander speedwell flourishing in the grass, marvellously delicate and blue with peeping white eyes. We passed over a petal-snow of hawthorn with the fragility of confetti carpeting the ground.

The bog, which Ida Holmes and I had gone to visit was "another world," a wet and wonderful water world strewn with water-loving plants beneath the alders. The bogbean was still in flower and we waded ankle-deep in water through large patches of bogbean leaves. For those who have never seen bogbean, its feathery flowers are perfection and more beautiful than many a wild orchid, each blossom washed with the faintest flush of pink and thickly covered with fringy plush of fine white threads. Its mauve-budded star-clusters have a beauty totally unmatched by its unprepossessing name, and rarely equalled in our native flora.

There were kingcups still in flower in the bog and we noted with delight their flat circular clusters of seed capsules, pinkish-green and ripe and fully open, and as pretty as any inflorescence. We passed vivid blue brooklime, orchid leaves polka-dotted with purple spots, adderstongue, minute forget-me-nots, and wood avens – its rosy-bells of peachy-pinkish-yellow tints nodding on their long stems.

The walk through this water wilderness was a joy rarely come across today, for here was the precious gift of nature, wild and rampant and beautiful, full of the wonder of life itself and disturbed only by a snipe concerned about our presence in this little Eden.

*6 June 1988*

Kingcup *Caltha palustris*

# LEGENDS OF A FLOWER YOU CAN'T FORGET

*F*ORGET-ME-NOT! A name with pining appeal. Remember me! Do not forget me. How did our wild forget-me-nots acquire such a hauntingly beautiful name? Our ancestors did not know these plants by that particular name. In fact they knew them as scorpion grasses or mouse-ear.

There are several legends associated with the naming of the forget-me-not. One of them tells of a knight who was strolling beside a river with the lady he loved.

On seeing some little blue flowers at the water's edge which she wished to possess, he plunged into the river and gathered them, but was borne away by the current and the weight of his armour.

As he sank he made one last effort before drowning and threw the flowers on the bank at her feet, crying plaintively: "Forget-me-not!"

Another legend tells of flowers having been given their names by the Creator. One little plant could not remember the name she had been given. On timidly asking the Creator what it had been, she was told: "Forget-me-not!"

Today I have been walking along the bed of the River Yare, where water forget-me-nots of the clearest blue flower along the river's edge. Water forget-me-nots are the most beautiful of all our native forget-me-nots.

Their tiny flower buds are pink, crowded together and are charmingly coiled, hence the old name of scorpion grass for the plant, because of the likeness of its inflorescences to the curved tail of a scorpion.

The pink buds open as pink flowers, then change to a clear blue with a bright yellow eye. This pretty colour-change of being pink in the bud, then blue when the flower is open is a curious characteristic of the Boraginaceae, or borage, family to which the forget-me-not belongs. It can be seen so prettily in viper's bugloss, another member of the family.

My visit to the river bed of the Yare had been a delightful experience. I walked out of the river carrying a stem of water forget-me-nots in order to write this column. Their liquid-blue petals, as though enamelled by some unseen hand, are quite unforgettable.

*18 July 1998*

Wood Forget-me-not *Myosotis sylvatica*

# BRIEF ESCAPE INTO WILDERNESS

*I*T is the middle of the afternoon and I am sitting in a favourite place… on an old wooden seat deep among the grasses in Hethel churchyard – God's untrimmed acre.

In this hallowed place there is peace and tranquillity, solitude and silence. Few would know of this churchyard, for the lane that leads to this church goes nowhere else in particular.

At my feet are bush vetches clustered with purple flowers being visited by bumblebees – experts in opening the pea-shaped blossoms. I notice some of their pollen baskets are laden, ready for the return trip to the nest.

The wind blows through the churchyard and all the moon-daisies and the grasses lean aslant gracefully. What a paradise for wild things is this consecrated place of straightened and tipsy tombstones. I leave the old wooden seat and wander round the churchyard. Everywhere there is wilderness. Eye-level wilderness. How we need wilderness in our root-starved lives.

I pass a thrush's anvil at the base of the walls of the church, scattered with the remains of prettily banded snails. I pass arching sprays of dog roses with pink-tipped buds. I stop to look at ground elder flowers, the leaves at one time considered such a delicacy – boiled like spinach and eaten with butter.

Enamel-blue damselflies are resting among the grasses, brilliant and delicately gauzy. I stop to smell huge flat creamy heads of elder flowers – their heavy-sweet musky scent so attractive to the senses. I notice there are banded snails among the cow parsley – the thrush with the anvil knows where to find its food!

Lacy umbels of hogweed smell strongly of the cow-house. A wren pierces the silence of the churchyard with its penetrating trilling. How aromatic are the leaves of ground-ivy, deep among the grasses. Waxy-chaliced buttercups gild the grasses here and there. What a sanctuary the churchyard is for the life of the wild.

The field maple in the church hedgerow is reddened with leaf galls, and leaf coils dangle from the hazels, the quaint little homes of the larvae of leaf-rolling weevils. Thistles near the church door, which is a riot of roses, are soon to be crowned with purple, and amethyst pincushions of field scabious are waiting in bud.

An angel among the grasses is encrusted with orange lichens. I remove some of the mosses at its base to find a clue to its age. The statue is dated, the Good Friday of 1914.

My forty minutes away from the world is over. I open the gate to leave the churchyard. It wails with a melancholy iron squeak, as it always has done. I close the gate and drop the latch. God's in his heaven in his untrimmed acre …

*18 June 1994*

# SPIRES AND CHALICES

*D*ETAILED study of the lives and waning fortunes of our wild flowers is a perennial passion of mine, so dearly cherished, as wilderness itself in nearly every form vanishes before our very eyes through man's destructive influences.

As I write this treasured nature note particularly with the hope that I may heighten levels of awareness, I am standing at the edge of a wood where there are many spires of bugle of the deepest mauvy-blue among a carpet of buttercups.

The chalices of the buttercups and the blue spires of the bugle are in strikingly beautiful contrast with one another.

Red campion is flowering among the bugle and the buttercups, and there are bright pink flowers of herb-robert, and half-blown dandelion clocks.

The bugle spires which are no more than a few inches apart soar through the blaze of buttercups, and they have many visitors including flies and bees and a green-veined white butterfly.

The stems of the bugle are square and hairy and of a mauvish-blue tint, and their purple-blue blossoms form dense and beautiful whorls crowded together up the flower-spikes.

Each little blue flower in the whorls is two-lipped and rather like a tiny trumpet, the upper lip vestigial, and the lower lip large, with blue side-lobes, prettily streaked with purplish-blue.

Inside are matching stamens and a long blue style, at the bottom of which is a green ovary, and outside there is the daintiest little cup of fused sepals. As I write these notes, there are bees visiting the bugle flowers, and I cannot but think that the blue world of the bugle spire, fashioned so perfectly, is the most beautiful place for a pollinating bee. Something else catches my eye before I close my nature notebook which is also interesting about the bugle spires – some of the leaves are almost as blue as the flowers.

I always feel that there is endless delight and a compelling fascination to be found in the world of wild flowers, and as I stand by the wood looking down on the blue spires of bugle among the buttercup chalices, each one a miracle of little petals evolved over hundreds of thousands of years, I think how sad it is that we are so careless of such a heritage of little gems, so forgetful of the flowers at our feet. Of wilderness itself. For what kind of wild world will we leave for others that preceding generations so enjoyed?

*11 June 1988*

# FLORAL PURPLE PROSE PASSAGES

WHEN I was at school, there was so much Shakespeare in our English literature classes, by the time I left there – Shakespeare was dead! However, time is a great healer, and today I have an affinity with Shakespeare which truly delights me. I have a love of wild flowers – and so had he.

The River Avon at Stratford and its flowery meadows in Shakespeare's day was only a few minutes' walk away from his childhood home. His environment must have been a wild and beautiful one which became deeply impressed on his mind.

For Shakespeare was familiar with the natural beauty of so many wild flowers, using his matchless gift of poetry to describe them, often in only two or three words. "Freckled cowslip" and "winking Mary-buds" are two delightful examples. It was not only wild flowers, though, to which his thoughts were attuned, for he had a love of herbs and garden flowers as well.

One of the best loved wild flower word-pictures of Shakespeare's comes from Love's Labour's Lost – "When daisies pied and violets blue, And lady-smocks all silver-white, And cuckoo-buds of yellow hue, Do paint the meadows with delight…" – cuckoo-buds being glossy-petalled buttercups, the yellow hue of the painted meadow coming from their waxy chalices.

Another word-picture perhaps delighted in just as much comes from A Midsummer Nights' Dream: "I know a bank whereon the wild thyme blows, Where ox-lips and the nodding violet grows…". Shakespeare's words concerning primroses have no equal – "pale primroses" (The Winter's Tale) and "faint primrose-beds" (A Midsummer Night's Dream), the word "faint" suggesting so delicately that sweet freshness of primroses in spring.

I have long loved Shakespeare's choice of words for describing cowslips – a flower mentioned by him at least six times – delighting with fairy-like charm in their details – "crimson drops" (Cymbeline) and "freckled cowslip" (King Henry V).

Violets, surely one of the best loved of all flowers, are referred to by Shakespeare on at least 18 occasions, the descriptive "nodding violet" of A Midsummer Night's Dream being perhaps the most beautiful.

Daisies are described in Cymbeline in a most delightful way – "let us find out the prettiest daisied plot we can…" – the daisied ground being for the grave of a dead youth. I have also long loved the phrase "And winking Mary-buds begin to ope their golden eyes" – an exquisite word-picture to be found in Cymbeline.

The poetic imagery is remarkable, and the words, matchless. It is thought that

Shakespeare was referring to the buds of kingcups, or marsh marigolds. In A Midsummer Night's Dream we find a wild flower called love-in-idleness. This is another, and very beautiful, name for the wild pansy also known as heartsease (Viola tricolor). Love-in-idleness – what dreamy thoughts that summons to the mind.

Lady's smock is one of my favourite wild flowers because of it's varying tints of mauve which range from deep lilac to almost white. It is thought that the name lady's smock was given to the flower because the lilac flowers, which look silver-white from a distance when carpeting a meadow, resembled the white smocks women used to spread out on the grass to bleach in the sun.

In Love's Labour's Lost, Shakespeare catches this exact impression of lady-smocks all silver-white. In a song of his, he also mentions maidens bleaching their summer smocks.

*January 1994*

A flowery meadow

# STARRY NATIVE OF DAMP WOODS

*T*HERE is an old proverb which goes like this – "Eat leeks in March and ramsons in May, and all the year after physicians may play."

John Gerard (1545-1612), barber-surgeon and botanist, whose Herbal epitomises Elizabethan botany, stated that: "In Britain, many labouring men of a strong constitution eat ramson leaves in April and May with butter. That portion of humanity who are delicate and more refined, leave the ramsons alone!" The plant was also used medicinally in brandy, and as a tonic in villages.

Ramsons are one of the beauties of the lily family (Liliaceae), a starry native of damp woods and shady places. In fact at one time there were unbroken acres of them in the wood behind our cottage. But in recent years hard core roadways have been put down for the removal of timber, which has destroyed what was "another world" with pathways for two feet through constellations of ramson flowers.

No plants were ever more a galaxy of earth-bound stars. In fact, I love ramsons. I love their starriness. I love their fragrant drift of garlic wherever one has walked among them. And I love their lily-of-the-valley type leaves.

The flower buds of ramsons, which are on long triangular stems, look rather like a laden spindle.

The two-lobed spathe of buds splits open with a burst of pure white stars – like a fairy bouquet of flowers.

Each flower consists of a six-rayed star of narrow pointed petals, with six white stamens in the middle, whose anthers tilt like see-saws across their slender filaments. Deep in the centre of the flower there is a green, three-celled ovary with one large seed in each cell.

All parts of ramsons smell of garlic.

Some people object to the scent but the fragrance released by the bruising of the leaves, while walking among them, I find delightful.

The name "ramson" is of great antiquity. In Anglo-Saxon times it was "hramsen", later ramsis then ramseys, and today, of course ramson.

Other names for the plant include wild garlic, bear's garlic, hog's garlic and gipsy onion, also fascinating "Devil's posy."

*15 May 1995*

Ramson *Allium ursinum*

# *Autumn*

*Why should you want? Behold the earth hath roots;*
*Within this mile break forth a hundred springs:*
*The oaks bear mast, the briars scarlet hips;*
*The bounteous housewife nature, on each bush*
*Lays her full mess before you.*

>            Timon of Athene
>            Act 4th. Scene 3rd.

# WOODLAND WALK

*T*HERE is something soothingly soft and persuasive about the voices of wood-pigeons, or ring-doves as they are also called.

"Put your shoes on Lucy, your shoes on Lucy, your…" they croon, with a sudden pause. A day or so before the recent hurricane with all its wind-burn and tree-toppling carnage, I went for a peaceful walk in a wood where the "coo-coooo-coooo-coo-coo" of wood-pigeons could be heard, crooning so gently, high up in the tree-tops.

Foxgloves were still in flower on a few leaning spikes, with little tumbles of leopard-spotted finger-bells. I passed a female holly with green berries, and a female yew – its rosy fruits, such a pretty contrast among the leafy needles of its dark foliage.

The papery fruit capsules of the bluebells were all empty, their black seeds gone. Everywhere I walked there were finely-spun spider nets pearled with graduated raindrops ringed with silvery light, like fairy hammocks of diamonds. I passed tree trunks tiled with ivy leaves, a spindle – a rosy-orange fire of dying leaves, its pink fruits with peeping orange seeds, and hawthorns crowded with crimson fruits.

I stood for a while by a pit at the edge of the wood, watching the mallard and moorhens. A grey squirrel came down an oak tree, head first, in jerks, filled with wary suspicion, and flashing its tail repeatedly, along with a storm of complaints about my motionless presence, orchestrated within seconds by the moorhens and ducks.

I waited for the water voles I had watched on other occasions, but they did not appear. On my way out of the wood I stopped to examine the fruits on a sweet chestnut tree. No nuts could have been better protected for their cases were lined with a pale green velvet of silky hairs, and they were wickedly prickly on the outside with an impenetrable husk of fine green needles.

I left the wood, returning at dusk when the cock pheasants were raucously going to roost, while a tawny-owl called in the distance. Bats were skimming the pit, twinned by the reflecting water. I visited the pit again a little before midnight. All was silent – as though waiting for tomorrow – except for a single raucous "krrrrrk" from a waterhen.

I walked through the wood in the dark, like a cat with velvet paws. For in such a place one becomes a very attentive listener – alert – for hidden secrets of the night.

*23 October 1987*

# FAIRY-LIKE FUNGI

$\mathcal{F}$UNGI are the most intriguing of living organisms, often fairy-like and appearing as though from nowhere overnight. They do not need sunlight. They have no chlorophyll.

Some of them have the most imaginative names, conjuring up curious images, such as beef-steak fungus, poison pie, earth stars, Jew's ear and dryad's saddle. There is also dead man's fingers, the destroying angel, ear-pick, bird's nest and candle-snuff fungus.

Lately, I have come across troop after troop of lawyer's wigs (*Coprinus comatus*), a most striking and distinctive fungus, seen in Fundenhall and, quite unforgettably, in the garden of The Vicarage at Tacolneston.

Here I was shown by the vicar, Simon Stephenson, a veritable pixie-land of lawyer's wigs, 70 of them scattered in troops and clusters – egg-shaped, busy-shaped, cylindrical, conical and bell-shaped – in fact, at every stage of their intriguing development.

All were shaggy with scales and just like lawyers' wigs: the bell-shaped ones the most mature, with deliquescing caps dissolving in their own juices – the sooty-black fluid dripping the spores into the soil while blackening surrounding vegetation.

The entire colony was weirdly beautiful and one of great charm, and one could not but wonder at the strange evolution of such remarkable organisms whose black juices were once used as inky fluid for writing.

Lawyers' wigs are quite capable of lifting tarmac, as occurred along a path in Ashwellthorpe last week when a stunning troop of lawyers' wigs suddenly appeared beside the road. Lawyers' wigs were eaten in Ancient Rome and today, some people consider them to rank among the most delicious of all toadstools.

If peeled when young and the stems discarded, they can be baked in the oven with breadcrumbs and cheese, cooked in stews or eaten raw in salads.

Fungi are the most fascinating of plants – some of them very strange indeed. Some are quaint, while others are beautiful despite their sinister charm. I much prefer fungi as natural history to look at and not as table delicacies to eat.

*9 October 1992*

Lawyers' Wig *Coprinus comatus*

# BEAUTY OF BUTTERFLIES

O F all the forms of life on this little planet of ours endlessly circling the sun in its milky whirl of gas and dust and stars, one of the most beautiful ever to emerge from evolution is the butterfly – a marvellously complex mass of molecules, its fairy-tale wings magically transformed from the body tissues of a caterpillar.

The sheer flimsiness and resplendency of these tiny environmental treasures evokes a profound sense of awe as one thinks about the hazardous adventure of their metamorphosis, and their evolutionary origins lost for ever across an inconceivable span of time.

It is tragic that so many of our butterflies are on the downward slope towards extinction, especially when there are only 66 different kinds in Britain including the migrants.

In spite of their decline we have just experienced a singularly beautiful "butterfly summer". The field at the back of our cottage, which is undergoing a slow transformation from arable land to meadow, has had many butterfly visitors over the last few months.

In fact, this summer the field has been a little seventh heaven particularly for wall butterflies, the tawny orange of their wings and the amethyst of thistle crowns being so beautiful together.

I have spent long periods watching the wall butterflies chasing one another, sipping nectar, and sweethearting together, their orange wings networked with brown and trimmed with little necklaces of eye-spots pinpointed with white pupils.

A dense stand of honey-scented thistle crowns at the edge of the field has been a great source of nectar for gatekeepers, and red admirals which are so vivid and velvety, peacocks, brimstones and charming little blues; as well as the walls and tortoiseshells, ringlets and coppers, their small spotted wings vividly orange and burnished so brightly.

It has been many years since I last saw such a feast of butterflies among so many flowerheads, their tongues, like watchsprings, uncurled, probing for nectar.

There is nothing quite like a dense stand of thistle crowns in the sunshine with their multitudes of mauve florets resplendent with the wings of butterflies.

And the most transfixing little scene of all is a butterfly settled on a honeyed flowerhead, the jewelled flicker of its parting wings like a flame burning fitfully.

*26 September 1989*

# MONSTER LOBSTER MOTH LOOKS LIKE DEAD LEAVES

*T*HERE are more than 2000 species of moths in Britain, and the larvae of the lobster moth are the most extraordinary of all British caterpillars.

Weird and crustacean-like, formidable in appearance, these awe-inspiring caterpillars are instantly identifiable. For, if threatened or while at rest, the lobster caterpillar raises its head and tail over its body in a strikingly defensive posture giving it a grotesque shape, not unlike a miniature lobster.

In fact no British caterpillar is more elaborately endowed for coping with disturbance from predators.

For there are also two diverging filaments at the end of its body which it can move about to make its threat display more elaborate, and glands below the thorax from which to squirt formic acid over parasites such as ichneumon flies, or small birds who might consider it an appropriate prey worth attacking.

What an intimidating defence strategy for a British caterpillar to face its world!

Those I have been rearing this summer looked remarkably like ants, in their early stages, the caterpillars in their first instar (development between moults) feeding solely on their discarded eggshells. Since then, they have been reared on beech leaves.

The caterpillars have been exciting to rear and riveting to watch, for they have prominent rows of conical humps along their backs giving them a dramatic outline, also long front legs, like those of a spider, which are neatly folded away when at rest, and an enormously enlarged tail segment which is swollen and arched forward over the back.

There is yet more to the lobster's extraordinary and extremely striking life history, for the moth, when at rest, perhaps on a beech twig, with its hindwings spread out below the forewings, resembles a bunch of dead leaves!

Just how has a caterpillar, like a lobster, with a moth camouflaged like a bunch of dead leaves, travelled down evolution's awesome vistas of time, and so intimidatingly?

Ruminating on such remote matters is fascinating and evokes a bewildering sense of wonder

*10 August 1996*

Lobster Moth Caterpillar
*Notodontidae: Stauropus fagi*

# A WALK IN THE WILDERNESS

As I write this note I am walking through 93 acres of woodland in Ashwellthorpe.

The sky above is cerulean and fleeced, with white clouds, It is a dazzlingly sunny day. A field maple is glowing with autumn gold, its amber-yellow leaves descending one by one to carpet the ground below.

The wood is very wet with rainwater pooled across my path. I stare downwards through its mirror-like surface which reflects to leafy perfection the arching branches soaring above. I turn over a hazel leaf. Clustered beneath it are 23 glossy red ladybirds. I eat a large juicy blackberry. The leaves on the bramble are tunnelled with whitish corridors curiously mined by the tiny caterpillars of a feathery moth prettily named – *Stigmella aurella*.

There are many green catkins tightly-clustered on the hazels – their dangling days still several months away.

Some of the green brambles are prettily spotted with crimson-staining rust fungus. I pass eye-catching twists of black bryony berries like red, green and orange beads threaded on a vine. I eat another blackberry. Ladybirds are sunning themselves on the dying foliage of hornbeam – its leaves so attractive with pleated veins and double-toothed edges. Clusters of leafy bracts filled with hornbeam nutlets lie on my pathway.

I pass leafy rosettes of wood spurge, and stop to stare at berries like ruby drops hanging from the stems of woody nightshade. Oval, ripe and glossy, how beautiful they are, threaded among the brambles. Hemp-agrimony seedheads are fluffy with parachute hairs, and wispy strands of honeysuckle, still budding with trumpets, hang from a hazel.

Chainsaws are whining in the wood as 12 acres of sycamore trees are felled and put through a chipping machine. I stop to stare at spindle berries as pink as sealing-wax, also scarlet hips like fairy light bulbs scattered along the arching spray of a dog rose. I pass bright pink flowers of common centaury and golden sprays of ragwort stars, also lawyers' wigs tiered with shaggy scales.

Nearby grows the death cap fungus – the deadly poisonous *Amanita phalloides*, also one of the most charming scatters of toadstools I have ever seen with pretty little mauve caps and fawn gills.

How wonderful it is to be mentally lost in the wilderness of this wood – nearly 1000 years after its inclusion in the Domesday Book. I wonder – who will be walking here 1000 years hence?

*6 October 1994*

## STROLLING ACROSS FEN IS ALWAYS A DELIGHT

$S$TRUMPSHAW Fen, a haven for wildlife of 746 acres, includes open water, reedbeds, woodland, marshland, wet meadow and alder carr – in fact a fascinating collection of Broadland habitats.

As I write this nature column I am rambling round this beautiful fen head-high in meadowsweet, common reed and the rosy-mauve flowers of great willowherb.

Here and there I can see yellow loosestrife in flower, a plant at one time bunched around the necks of draft animals as a repellent, "to loosen strife" caused by irritating insects.

Purple-loosestrife is also in bloom, its soaring spires richly whorled with magenta-coloured flowers.

I spend many moments of pleasure examining marsh pea (*Lathyrus palustris*), a "charmer" with winged stems and tendrils scrambling among neighbouring plants. Every year I visit Strumpshaw specially to delight in this rarity of fens and marshes, for its "sweet pea flowers" of clear mauve are quite enchanting. Near the marsh pea, a large emperor moth caterpillar is at rest on a stem of meadowsweet. Milk parsley is in flower, the foodplant of the caterpillar of the swallowtail butterfly which lives on the fen.

I pass snow-white trumpets of bellbine, its flower buds furled like an umbrella, and tufted vetch, streaked with purple and blue flowers, scrambling among the common reeds. On many of the hogweed heads there are soldier beetles, so called because of their colourful resemblance to 19th century military uniforms.

There are reed-fringed dykes either side of my pathway in which I can hear tantalising plops. I stop to finger through tansy, releasing the aromatic oils in the glands in its leaves.

As the wind hisses through the reeds, I can see floating green carpets of duckweed. Gliding over the fen is a female marsh harrier. She is dark brown with cream-coloured shoulders. Her wingspan, difficult to judge, is probably between three and four feet.

I cut across the fen where there are white water-lilies in flower – at one time a source for oils and distillations used by apothecaries.

Back where I began my ramble, I walk across a busy railway line in order to leave the fen. Penalty for not shutting the gates beside the railway – £50!

*13 August 1997*

Milk Parsley *Peucedanum palustre*

# SONG ON THE WING

*T*HIS summer, while out in the lanes in the village, I have often paused to marvel over the silvery chains of song, sustained for minutes on end in the sky above me: songs poured out most exquisitely from the tiny syrinxes (vocal organs) of skylarks.

How truly remarkable it is that a bird should sing on the wing and mark out a territory below with such fluency, by soaring, circling and singing above it, as though perched on a song-post high in the sky.

No wonder the skylark, a vocal speck in the blue, has attracted the attention of composers and poets; for what perfection there is in those words of William Shakespeare – "Hark! hark! the lark at heaven's gate sings".

And what lyrical perfection there is in the notes of Vaughan Williams' "miniature violin concerto" – The Lark Ascending, a musical romance born from a literary idea of George Meredith's.

Meredith, in his poem The Lark Ascending, speaks of the bird as "ever winging up and up". And, "He drops the silver chain of sound, of many links without a break"; precisely what the skylarks have been doing so beautifully this summer, soaring above the open fields.

The skylark's nest-cup of grass and roots is always on the ground, built into a little depression of hollow, even hoof-prints left behind by cattle, the nest perhaps partly concealed in a tussock of grass.

Open countryside is the home of the skylark – farmland, grassland, meadows, moors, commons and even sand-dunes; a single pair may raise as many as three broods in a summer. While I have been out in the lanes over the last few weeks, the sky has been strangely silent, not a silvery sound from on high anywhere.

For now is the time when skylarks moult and renew their plumage, their silvery songs ceasing.

Man's atrocities where nature is concerned are quite unbelievable. For less than 100 years ago, these soaring songsters, rising and descending with their silvery chains of sound, were netted on the South Downs and shipped across the Channel to French markets as food.

Amazingly, Britain, now a country of bird-watchers and bird protection, had a thriving export trade with France in dead skylarks.

*9 September 1992*

# FLOWERS BY THE SEA

*L*IVING inland as I do, the shifting world of the sand dune is not a very familiar place to me. Recently I went for a walk with John Brown of Ormesby St Michael to look at the plant life on the sand dunes at Caister.

The dunes, which lie parallel to the sea behind a vast stretch of shore, are loosely-thatched with marram grass whose stiff leaves and penetrating root systems trap the sands blown inland from the shore. I was delighted to see the haze of sheep's-bit in misty-blue among the marram tufts. Trumpeting among the dunes was sea bindweed, a plant with trails of little leaves and large striped bell-flowers of ever-deepening pink the further the eye travels down the trumpet.

We delighted in the pea-shaped flowers of the restharrow so pink and pretty, sea sandwort so neatly-leaved, and yellow rattle, as we walked over dunes mined during the last war. In the sandy hollows there were yellow fires of lady's bedstraw.

We crossed the shore and returned over the palest of golden sands strewn with bluish pebbles. Here, among trails and concentrations of little arrow-shaped footprints, we looked with amazement at a ringed plover's nest.

Indiscernible among pebbles in a slightly sandy hollow, were three clay-coloured eggs marked with dark flecks, encircled with bits of shingle debris.

Fascinated by the hazardous situation of the nesting site, we walked away to watch from a distance the return of the ringed plover – or stone-runner as it is locally known – which lives so dangerously, running along like a pebble on legs back to its nest, the open sandy-stoney camouflage of the beach unbelievably concealing.

We returned to the sand dunes and stopped to look at the sea-green thistly-blue sea hollies, downy-soft hare's-foot clover, and bird's-foot-trefoil in vivid yellow patches, blue with sheep's-bit among which a six-spot burnet was hovering.

We returned to the place where we had started this delightful walk – the magic of nature among these arid dunes, etched in the memory for many days to come.

*13 August 1991*

Lesser Bindweed *Convolvulus arvensis*

# AMAZING WORLD OF WILD BIRDS

It is not very often, with my overriding love of botany, that I go bird watching, but when I do, I usually go to Cley. Birdwatchers have an unparalleled degree of commitment that rarely comes across in other fields, and their equipment and hushed absorption in the bird hides is a subject for study all on its own.

The other day I set out at 8.30 on a beautiful blue morning to join a group of naturalists "going round Cley" – which means walking along the East Bank considered to be the most famous bird walk in Britain, walking along an enormous steeply shelving shingle bank, and entering bird hides on 400 acres of marshes.

The marshes include brackish marsh (fresh and salt water mixed), freshwater marsh (spring fed), and saltwater marsh (tidal); and the bird hides, which all have their own names, are discreet wooden shelters with seating ranged against long horizontal letter-box slits, for observing unobserved a riveting assortment of birds.

On my way to the first hide I stopped to look at a painted lady visiting a dazzlingly beautiful patch of fleabane gilded with daisy disks. Seated in the hide I had the most absorbing view of snipe with handsome striped backs, and long straight bills probing in a shallow pool of water. I also watched dunlins, a ruff and a curlew, among whom I was amazed to see several jackdaws.

On my way to the East Bank, I did what I always do – I stopped to listen to the sound of the wind, that wild and elusive spirit of Norfolk hissing through the reedbeds. Before I reached Bittern hide I paused for a few moments to look at the sea asters, and to stare at their beautiful starry heads of milky-mauve daisies. Seated in the hide overlooking a pool furrowed by warm breezes I watched green sandpipers and several more snipe.

On my way to the next hide – Teal hide – I passed some woody nightshade, its threading stems bearing trusses of glossy red berries and purple flowers. Here I stopped to look at a cormorant with big black webbed feet, and with its wings – which never fail to amaze me – hanging out to dry. In Teal hide I had a most delightful view of black-tailed godwits on long stilty legs, an avocet, and some ringed plovers – who are the most engaging, nobby little birds with black and white rings round their necks.

I drove home – my head full of Cley and its amazing waterworld of wild birds, a wintering ground for some, a breeding sanctuary for others, and an "international airport" of avian renown.

*21 September 1988*

# A HORNET'S NEST

WHAT, I wonder, is your reaction to the word "hornet" as you start to read this article? Or put a little differently, why is it that the hornet strikes terror into the hearts of so many people, which is totally out of proportion and completely at variance with the nature of the insect?

Hornets do not seek trouble. They are mild tempered, even good tempered. They are far less aggressive than common wasps, and will not sting unless seriously provoked. "Stirring up a hornets' nest" is a slanderous reference to the hornet.

It does it great injustice. Recently Tom Dennett of Denton Lodge, Feltwell, invited me to look at a hornets' nest on his farm.

The nest had been built hanging from the roof, inside a small chicken hut. When I arrived there, it had fallen from the roof on to its side on the floor, but it was "business as usual" for the hornets, whether suspended from the roof or lying on the floor.

The nest had been beautifully constructed in horizontal swirls of paper, made by scraping wood from trees and other timber and pulping it with saliva.

The place was quite literally buzzing with hornets.

We filmed the hornets and their nests only inches away from them, and at no time was there any cause for alarm, the hornets passing round one's head, like traffic negotiating a roundabout.

All inhabitants of a hornets' nest, males and workers, die by November, except the fertile queens hibernating in sheltered places such as a hollow tree. When spring comes each one searches for a nesting site and founds a new colony.

Hornets, which in my opinion are rather handsome, are far from commonplace, in fact they have become rather rare, probably due to senseless persecution and loss of old trees in which to nest.

In the 36 years we have lived in our cottage in Ashwellthorpe, there have always been hornets, either in the hollow oaks at the edge of the meadow behind the cottage, or in the wood behind the meadow. How pleased I am to know that there are hornets in Feltwell too!

*11 October 1997*

Hornet's nest *Vespa crabro*

# DISCOVER A WILDLIFE GEM

THE Yare Valley Walk, a gem of four-and-a-half miles, skirts the southern edge of Norwich.

Here, marshes and meadows, reedbed and woodland, and a wealth of water-loving plants lie relatively undisturbed, the River Yare winding its way along the length of the walk.

A few days ago I went for a riverside ramble along part of the Yare Valley Walk.

I began my walk beside the old bridge at Cringleford, built over the river in the early 16th century, damaged by floods in 1519 and subsequently rebuilt.

Wild angelica was in flower along the riverside, its dusky-pink umbels, in which ladybirds and wasps were foraging, so soft to the touch.

The plant has rather a beautiful name – derived from angelic or heavenly properties once attributed to it. I stopped to look at fleabane, golden with daisy disks, its leaves used for centuries, as its name implies, as a flea repellent.

Water forget-me-nots with liquid-blue petals were flowering among duckweed. Here, the surface of the River Yare was glassy and beautiful and gracefully overhung with grey-green willows.

I stopped to talk to two anglers, one of whom showed me a perch he had caught, pulling up a frill of spines along the centre of its back.

The fish, which had orange fins and dark vertical stripes along its side, and a strong spine on the gill cover, was returned to the River Yare. Also in the river, I was told, there were bream, roach, tench and pike; rudd, dace and gudgeon. Bellbine was in flower in many places along the riverside – its trumpet-shaped flowers of a brilliant snowy-white.

Also along the river's edge was water mint in aromatic whorls of lilac flowers. A plant with many old medicinal uses, water mint was at one time used as a form of smelling salts.

Here I stopped to look at overhanging alders and leaning willows, deeply and beautifully reflected in the River Yare, the wind at times ruffling the surface like the strokes of an impressionist's paintbrush. I passed water figwort, purple bells of comfrey, and meadowsweet, also gipsywort tightly-whorled with little white flowers.

A strong black dye was at one time produced from gipsywort and used for daubing the body to give swarthy looks to vagabonds masquerading as fortune-tellers.

Once again I stopped along my pathway to look at the river, the wind silvering the surface with shoals of broken lights.

The flower-heads of a bed of common reed were a beautiful reddish-purple, and in the distance there were regal displays of purple-loosestrife.

Yellow water-lilies were still in flower along the river, their brandy bottle seed-capsules protruding from the surface.

Here I stopped to watch the river going by, the passing clouds above me fleecily mirrored in its surface.

I crushed lesser water-parsnip to release its distinctive smell, and paused to admire a stretch of marsh woundwort, its pretty mauve whorls, a delight to the eye. I discovered trifid bur-marigold growing near the river bank, a plant I have not seen for many years, also common meadow-rue.

At the end of my riverside walk I stopped to talk to another angler who informed me of other fish to be found in the River Yare including the miller's thumb, carp, and occasionally the nine-spined stickleback and eels. My Yare Valley Walk had been delightful, head-high in the wilderness at times, and with so many different habitats to enjoy – marshland, meadow, woodland and reedbed, and of course the fascination of the River Yare.

*14 September 1996*

Riverside walk

# HOPALONG INSECTS

$\mathcal{F}$ROGHOPPERS, so-called because of their sloping appearance and jumping ability, are some of the quaintest insects in Britain. The wings of the adults slant down their backs like a little shallow pitched roof, and the distance they can hop is staggering.

This appealing little insect, of which we have ten different kinds, is better known in its nymph stage when blowing bubbles on all sorts of plants, including docks and grasses.

The nymphs have a tiny valve at their tail-ends which lets air in or out. Fluids sucked from plants pass through the nymph's digestive system forming a film across the valve.

The film is blown into bubbles by air expelled through the valve, forming the familiar blobs of bubbly froth we call cuckoo-spit, or spittle.

I quite often look inside cuckoo-spit to see "who is living there," and usually find a slippery green or brown froghopper nymph, or spittle bug, about a quarter of an inch long.

These white frothy homes in which the nymphs immerse themselves, and which I have watched being built on plants in our kitchen, prevent dessication and protect them from predators, though certain solitary wasps have learned that there is a meal inside the bubbles and they seize the nymphs from the cuckoo-spit to feed their own young.

Cuckoo-spit is an old country name given to the froth because it begins to appear on plants about the time the cuckoo arrives. The cuckoo-spit gets larger as the nymph grows until it eventually moults leaving the bubble foam as an adult froghopper.

Recently, just before dusk, I was examining the vegetation round the edge of the field behind our cottage. There was a flowery stand of thistles and in it were metallic-blue damselflies, ladybirds, bumblebees and hoverflies – all at rest for the night.

Among them were adult froghoppers, nearly half an inch long, conspicuously patterned in black and red – the only brightly coloured species we have in Britain.

I wanted to look at their spiny back legs under magnification, and they proved very difficult to catch with such powerful hind legs leaping three or four feet at the slightest disturbance.

The nymphs of the black and red froghopper, unlike others we see, live underground sucking juices from roots, surrounding themselves with froth in the soil; the adult, which is so handsome, lives above the ground.

*2 August 1989*

# MAGIC APPEAL OF MOUSE'S HOME

*I* have never forgotten the first time I saw a mouse. I was two or three years old at the time. And I do not know whether it was a wood mouse or a house mouse, as both enter houses.

I went into the larder with my mother, and there on the sill was the cucumber dish, and in the dish, a whole cucumber, and sitting on the cucumber a mouse enjoying its new-found food! The story of this little scene and the shock of delight it caused was repeated many times down the years.

To this day I still delight in mice, whether wood, house or harvest mice, and of course all the other mousy mammals that go along with them such as field voles, bank voles and shrews with snipy noses.

A few months ago, a study was built onto our cottage. Existing gutters were taken down along with a number of little wire balloon-guards from the tops of rainwater down-pipes; badly worn balloon-guards being discarded, and one in good condition being set aside for re-use. The balloon-guard was temporarily housed in a box in the garden containing small garden tools and bulbs.

While sorting through the box recently I noticed with sheer astonishment that the balloon-guard had been requisitioned for housing. I picked up the guard which contained the most delightful little mouse nest I had ever seen and put a finger down the entrance hole. No one was at home! What a remarkable place I thought – of all mousy places – in which to build a nest!

How clever, and how resourceful of the mouse. But, just how had the mouse pictured the balloon-guard's potential, which must have caused quite an inquisitive investigation before any decision concerning its use as a nesting site was actually made? The nest fitted the inside of the spherical drain-guard exactly, the security of the wire guard being perfect. The mouse was safe!

There was only one entrance to the nest between two of the wires which were slightly bent apart, which of course the mouse had noticed. The nest was built of countless little pieces of grass, straw and shredded brown paper; dead leaves, a shredded plastic bag and the pets column from the *Eastern Daily Press* which had lined the tool box.

*12 June 1993*

# ADVENTURES OF BETTY BEETLE

Once upon a time Betty Beetle lived in a water-butt. How she became domiciled in such a strange place is something of a mystery – for a lid closed down over her water-home.

So runs what could be a tale told to children… A few days ago, Pat and Gordon Mills of Tharston telephoned me about a female great diving water beetle living in their water-butt. They had opened the lid of the butt to reach for some water and, with a little shrink of horror, had seen a strange creature diving from the surface of the water to the floor of the butt. They had borrowed a book from their neighbours and had identified the beetle quite correctly.

However, they wished to clean out the water-butt and had asked for my assistance in removing and re-housing the water beetle, one of the largest in Britain. As sometimes happens, though they wished the beetle to have a more appropriate home, Mrs Mills had become quite attached to her, actually naming her Betty Beetle. So Betty Beetle was removed from the premises making me feel more than a little like an undertaker.

Betty Beetle, at the time of writing this note, is living in an aquarium on our kitchen window ledge, containing a bucketful of fascinating pond water full of vegetation and animal life obtained from a pit in our village, in which there is no farm run-off. She is a very lively beetle with grooved wing-cases and yellow margins, either busy dredging through the pond deposits in the bottom of the tank, or suspended diagonally just beneath the surface of the water with the tip of her abdomen protruding through the duckweed.

Her powerful hind legs are fringed with long hairs which spread out when she swims, rather reminding me of feathering with oars. When the beetle is still, her hind legs are kept high, curved above the other pairs of legs which hang downwards.

Great diving water beetles are exciting creatures to watch. But they are rapacious carnivores preying on any small water creature such as a tadpole, or even a small fish.

They are best not handled, or handled very carefully, for they have a pair of sharp spikes on their undersides and a defense mechanism which produces nerve poison, sufficiently lethal to kill a frog. A fascinating beetle, yes, but something to be reckoned with if you happen to be a different kind of water creature. In fact if I were a tadpole I certainly would not want to meet a great diving water beetle! Betty Beetle is to be re-homed yet again in a pit within a little wilderness in our village. And that is the end of the tale of Betty Beetle and the water-butt.

*15 June 1993*

# FLOWER POWER AGAINST THE FLEA MENACE

*I*T may surprise readers to know that there are 47 different kinds of fleas in Britain whose adults are parasitic on birds and mammals whose blood they suck.

The largest British flea is the mole flea, and there is the familiar dog flea and, of course, the rabbit flea, the carrier of myxomatosis. From time immemorial fleas must have been a problem to man – on his animals, his pets in his home and on himself.

In Tudor times the floors of houses, especially when entertaining, were often strewn with freshly cut meadowsweet, or rushes and herbs with sweet-smelling grasses.

For fragrant plants were a favourite means of masking 16th-century smells. They also contained fleas!

For centuries fleabane (the bane of fleas) was highly prizes as a natural insecticide, the vapour given off when the leaves were dried and burned being used to drive away fleas. Even in its unburned state the plant was dried and sprinkled as an insecticide.

Whether fleabane, if tested today, would live up to its name I do not know.

The scientific name was given to fleabane by Linnaeus (1707-1778), Swedish biologist, not only where the matter of fleas were concerned, but also because he had been told by a General Keit in the Russian army that his men, when marching against the Persians, cured themselves of dysentery with fleabane.

The plant is also known by the name of Job's tears because it was believed that Job used it to cure his ulcers. A few days ago while driving through Forncett St Mary I came across a most attractive stretch of fleabane growing alongside great willowherb, water mint and meadowsweet.

The fleabane was covered with golden-yellow buttons. Each flower consisted of a central disc of closely-packed florets surrounded by a flat fringe of ray florets. The central disc was a lovely tint of deep gold, the encircling fringe, bright yellow.

Fleabane, which is very leafy, grows in damp grassy places such as waysides, in wet meadows, on marshy ground, by riversides, along banks of streams, and in ditches. The Romans thought fleabane very attractive and used if for making wreaths.

*12 September 1998*

Fleabane *Pulicaria dysenterica*

# SEXTON BEETLES

$C$HARLES Darwin, that great Victorian naturalist, said: "Whenever I hear of the capture of rare beetles, I feel like an old war horse at the sound of a trumpet!"

I know a little of the excitement he felt, for our cottage abuts many acres of deciduous woodland, and quite often interesting beetles, drawn by the bright lights, wander about outside the back door at night.

Most of the beetles end up living in boxes on the kitchen table, for the best way to pick up knowledge is to live in close contact with them. The other night while shutting up the hens after dark, I noticed an enormous jet-black beetle trapped in the hens' water bowl, feebly treading water in its death throes.

I dried the beetle, which had long spiny legs and dull orange tips to its antennae, and put it in a box with plenty of wild vegetation. In a little while it had recovered – and had become alert and lively, and I noticed that here were a number of tiny fawn mites running about under its chin.

The head and thorax of the beetle were shiny and the wing cases ridged and pitted and rather dull. Its body measured 1¼ inches and it buzzed protestingly when handled and unfolded enormous gauzy wings.

But the most interesting thing of all about these intimidating-looking beetles are their macabre habits, for they are the grave-diggers and undertakers of the insect world. Even their Latin name – Nicrophorus – means "grave-digger," though they are more commonly known as burying beetles or sexton beetles, the last name being remarkably apt when one thinks of church sextons whose duties once included digging graves.

These sexton beetles locate by scent carcases ready for committal, perhaps a dead bird, mouse or mole, and they scrape away the earth underneath the bodies so that they gradually sink into the excavated cavity, the corpses then being used by the beetles as future food for their offspring.

My burying beetle, which I have now released in order that it may continue with its habit of tidying up the countryside, was fed on tinned kitten food while in captivity – a pet food it greatly liked.

Although quite common in Britain, these amazing little funeral directors of the insect world are seldom seen for they fly at night and lie low in the daytime.

*1 July 1987*

# STIFFKEY SALTMARSH

*R*ECENTLY, while botanising in North Norfolk, I fell in love with Stiffkey saltmarsh, and with its marvellous amethyst carpet of sea lavender stretching far away into the mauve distance under a rainy-grey sky.

Here along this fascinating coastline 500 acres of riveting saltmarsh stretch from Morston marshes in the east – through Stiffkey – to Wells in the west.

Stiffkey saltmarsh forms part of a complex of tidal saltmarsh, creeks and mudflats, and this totally absorbing place, scheduled grade I, SSSI, is one of the largest surviving areas of natural saltmarsh in Britain. I spent many happy hours botanising through the marshes, spellbound by the mauviness of the sea lavender mixed with little drifts of silvery aromatic sea wormwood, or southernwood.

Crested along the muddy creeks I discovered sea purslane with flowering spikes of dulled-gold among its silvery foliage. And botanising, ever seawards, I eventually reached a ridge with a pathway along it, where sea rocket was in bloom with curious swollen fruits and pretty lilac flowers, so resembling the more delicate blossoms of lady's smock.

Beyond the ridge there was a vast expanse of samphire, which looked as though many acres of sticky mud had undergone mini afforestation with countless succulent, skimpy little fir trees, growing among the winding creeks and muddy water channels. Beyond the samphire and still stretching towards the sea, were many acres of wet, rippled sand, crunchy with shells and coiled with lugworm casts.

And beyond all these fascinating habitats – with the roar of the sea in the far distance – were family parties raking in the wet sandy mud for cockles, which they dug out just below the surface by the bucketful to be taken home and boiled for supper that night. I turned round to face the Stiffkey coastline, 1½ miles away, and I retraced by steps across the mudflats, through the samphire, stepping precariously over many sinuous mud-sucking water channels, and back across those idyllic amethyst saltmarshes.

What a day it had been. All mud and magic. And a place – just for once – where man had not sinned against the environment.

*29 August 1987*

Sea Lavender *Limonium vulgare*

# MEADOW LAMENT

*I* remember a countryside enriched by farming, where natural meadows and natural pastures, mown for hay or grazed by livestock, were commonplace.

Nowadays, it is difficult to find a field with a natural crop of flowering plants at all.

Today's agricultural grassland, comprising little besides rye grass fertilised for vigorous growth, is just another crop as sterile as a golf course.

Natural flower-rich meadows do still exist, and are treasures that need a certain amount of grazing or cutting to prevent a natural succession of scrub, saplings, trees and woodland.

The other day I went to Gressenhall to look at one of these old meadows. It was a masterpiece of wild flowers like those of my childhood.

I walked through the meadow "floodlit inside" with a special kind of joy that such a thick mosaic of wild flowers still existed.

The meadow, which covered five acres, had hedgerows of tall trees including crab apples, oaks and hollies, wreathed about with honeysuckles.

During the summer the meadow "is left to itself", but for the rest of the year it is grazed by four ponies.

I was told that years ago, when Gressenhall Museum was a workhouse, an old grey pony, which took the laundry basket from the workhouse to Dereham and back, used to graze on this beautiful meadow.

Prudence and Ronald Wright, of Beck Farm, took me through the meadow which was yellow with buttercups, red with clover and rich with yellow rattle.

I had never seen so much bog pimpernel before, a spongy carpet of diminutive flowers among marsh pennywort leaves.

This jewel of a meadow where snipe nest contains many orchids. Knee-deep in flowers we wandered through tufted vetch, selfheal and amethyst whorls of water mint; ragged-robin, both pure white and bright pink; fleabane and creamy foams of meadowsweet along with wild angelica, great willowherb, marsh bird's-foot-trefoil and sneezewort. A shallow drain dug many years ago was white with marsh bedstraw.

I left this flower meadow, relieved that it had never been destroyed by development, or drained and cultivated for agricultural purposes.

Our few remaining unploughed meadows must not face extinction. Friendly farming, somehow, must prevail.

*13 September 1991*

# BABBLING BROOK

A few days ago, I went for a walk with Ida Holmes who is a right-holder and protector of Flordon Common – a site of special scientific interest (SSSI) – where no operation that could be damaging, can be carried out without prior consultation with the Nature Conservancy Council.

I went to Flordon to botanise along a charming little tributary of the River Tas which borders the south side of the common.

Here we found patches of selfheal with bright purple flowers once used to heal the wounds inflicted by sickles and scythes. Growing alongside were charming little groups of eyebright, still used as any eye lotion, whose petals were so sweetly appealing with their tiny yellow landing stages and streaky purple honey-guides for pollinating insects.

A little further on we stopped to study the brook, its running water, silvery with broken light, and its little voice tinkling and plopping over the stony bed below.

Nearby there were hover-flies, honeybees and a handsome yellow and black longhorn beetle, feasting on the deep pink blackberry blossoms. Upright hedge-parsley, diminutive and charming with dainty mauve umbels, was growing by the brambles.

We walked a little further and stopped again to listen to the brook, its voice making such a pretty noise babbling along beside us. Here we met a beautiful stretch of hemp agrimony, its flowerheads fluffy with styles and busy with hover-flies.

Butterflies twinkled among the golden stars of ragwort and the many amethyst heads of water mint, smothered with protruding stamens. The brook, silvered with broken ripples and babbling with mellow tinkles, flowed on. Alongside we noticed spellbinding enamel-blue flowers of water forget-me-not with tiny pink buds furled in green coils.

As we paused to look at water figwort and the little yellow marigold faces of fleabane, we could hear the brook gurgling and plopping behind the vivid spires of purple loosestrife. We measured alders growing along the brook-side, some with circumferences of five to six feet, and we looked at great willowherb with its flowers of purplish-rose, each with its eye-catching creamy-coloured cruciform stigma.

Listening to the muted music of the brook as it dropped over the stones on its way to the distant sea, had been a delight with Ida Holmes – whose family have lived in this idyllic place since 1813, and who, so greatly to her credit, is the most indefatigable guardian of this SSSI.

*24 August 1987*

# HAVENS OF WILDLIFE IN OUR VERGES

WHAT is a hedgerow? What is a verge? One is a narrow strip of woodland, the other is a belt of vegetation, both contribute to a wayside which often consists not only of a grassy verge and a hedgerow but also of a ditch and its banks, which we seldom, if ever, look at.

The roads of Britain were in a bad state by the 18th century abounding with mud and potholes, noted contemporary writers. When road construction by men such as McAdam was introduced, highways became narrower as it was no longer necessary for vehicles to take wide berths to avoid major hazards.

The ground between the edge of the road and the boundary hedge became wider and colonised by plants giving rise to verges.

With so much wildlife driven out of the fields by intensive agriculture today, these verges have become significant "nature reserves" ribboning over Britain providing essential habitats for plants, animals and insects, amounting to about 240,000 acres in England and Wales.

Different soils along different verges often support different floras. Even a sunny aspect can make a difference to the type of plants found growing there, south-facing verges being far more interesting than north-facing ones.

It is curious how our waysides are regarded by many people as places of little significance, when they have become so important a habitat for conservation.

For those who enjoy walking and have an interest in the life of the wayside, it will be noticed that umbellifers dominate grassy verges with lacy displays of tiny white flowers. Cow parsley foams from April until June giving way to rough chervil in June and July then upright hedge-parsley from July until September.

Many plants can be enjoyed in our waysides at the moment, red campion and white campion. Red campion has no fragrance while white campion is scented in the evening attracting night-flying moths.

There are also large white patches of bladder campion along our waysides, emitting a clove-like scent at night. Easily recognised, their sepals are joined together and inflated like a balloon or bladder behind the flower.

Meadow buttercups, identified by spreading sepals as the flowers open, are now common on our roadsides, and so are ox-eye daisies, marguerites or moon-daisies, which transform grassy waysides with their beauty.

In lanes with damp soil, patches of comfrey can sometimes be found with the most attractive blue and reddish-purple flowers much loved by bumblebees. There are several pretty vetches flowering along the verges too, including common vetch with magenta-coloured blossoms usually in pairs, and the beautiful tufted vetch which scrambles by means of branched tendrils, and which has long spikes of bright, bluish-purple flowers.

Field poppies are just beginning to appear along the verges, and so is common mallow with its prettily-streaked rosy-mauve flowers. Bird's-foot-trefoil, also known as bacon-and-eggs, can also be found along the edge of the roadside.

In the hedgerows behind the verges sweetly-scented honeysuckle and arching sprays of dog roses are coming into flower.

Verges, which are important as reservoirs for plants, animals, birds and insects, need sensitive management. For they are not just green fringes to the tarmac, but bastions for disappearing wildlife against extermination.

*13 June 1998*

Umbellifers

# AMAZING MECHANISMS

*M*ANY of us enjoy looking at flowers. Some of us even notice the leaves, but, how often do we examine their seed dispersal mechanisms?

Plants use a fascinating variety of strategies for distribution of their fruits and seeds.

Some of them, such as cleavers or goosegrass, produce fruits with numerous hooks, rather like Velcro, which hitch a ride by clinging on to clothing, or to the fur of passing animals.

Others use water to float their fruits, such as yellow water lilies whose brandy-bottle-shaped seed capsules are kept afloat by air spaces in their tissues, while moving on the water to a new flowering site.

Yet others use wings and a ride on the wind to disperse their seeds, such as sycamore and field maple, silver birch and ash.

Many seeds are dispersed undigested by passing through animals and birds, the soft, outerparts of berries, for example, having provided a nourishing meal first.

Hazel nuts, known as dry fruits, are successfully dispersed, perhaps by squirrels storing them for the winter who subsequently forget their locations! The same applies to acorns buried by jays.

Some plants such as hairy bittercress, a common wild plant in gardens, use explosive mechanisms to shower their seeds over the garden.

Gorse pods, when dry, burst with a sharp crack and twist violently to eject their seeds on hot summer days. In fact many members of the pea family have explosive pods.

There are other plants which "do it themselves" most intriguingly such as the group known as the stork's-bills which have fruits like a long narrow beak.

The beak, or bill, when ripe splits into five narrow strips with a seed attached to each segment or tail. Each tail twists into a corkscrew. I have often watched this mechanism with amazement when common stork's-bill has been on the kitchen window ledge above the sink.

With changes in humidity the corkscrew tail either screws itself up more tightly or unwinds, the seed with its tail unbelievably travelling across the window ledge on its own, by its twisting movements, till it buries itself down the crack at the back of the ledge, ready for germination!

Another method of seed dispersal which intrigues me, is the circular gallery of holes which appears immediately below the disc of radiating stigmas on top of the seed capsule of the field poppy. This amazing little "pepper-pot" releases its numerous seeds a few at a time through the gallery of holes, when buffeted by the wind.

*1 November 1994*

# NATURE'S CLOCKS

Υ ESTERDAY I wrote about the fascinating variety of strategies, or ingenious mechanisms, used by plants for the dispersal of their fruits and seeds.

These included hooks for clinging on to the fur of passing animals, wings that spin – for a free ride on the wind, the alimentary tracts of birds and animals, and self-dispersal by explosive seed pods. Another method of seed dispersal, most exquisitely made, is the equipping of seeds with a parachute constructed of downy hairs like spun glass or gossamer.

The most spectacular and beautiful of all parachutes are those crafted by nature into clocks – the dandelion, goat's-beard, also known as Jack-go-to-bed-at-noon, and salsify, all bearing fruiting heads in the form of downy clocks.

Recently, Jack Brighton of Queen Elizabeth Drive, Beccles, sent me several stems picked from a strange plant which had appeared in his garden, and which he and others had not been able to identify. The plant is called purple salsify, introduced into Britain from France and Italy around 1700, grown in gardens, with its taproots being used as a vegetable. It is now naturalised in meadows and along roadsides.

I put the salsify in water and one of the fruiting heads has since opened into a handsome fawn-coloured clock of feathery parachutes, nearly four inches in diameter. Salsify and goat's-beard, to which it is related, produce the biggest wild seed clocks in Britain.

The seed clock of goat's-beard is three inches in diameter and white, and as with salsify the parachutes all fit together in an exquisitely spherical fruiting head. To me, the most beautiful of all our seed clocks is that of the dandelion, a miracle of flimsy architecture, its parachutes fitting together in a downy ball of exquisite intricacy.

Every dandelion clock… a marvel of natural design. Every parachute set free from the intricate realm of the clock… a marvel of gossamer hairs. Every dandelion seed… a traveller in the wind, suspended on down, embarking on its journey… the marvel of life. What a piece of work is a seed clock. How has such architecture ever come about?

*2 November 1994*

Dandelion clocks *Taraxacum officinale*

# A FRAGRANT, FEATHERY BEDSTRAW

*H*OW I love the fires of lady's bedstraw sweeping along the verges at the moment. In fact, lady's bedstraw, so delicate and dainty in every way, is the prettiest of all the bedstraws native to Britain, of which we have a least 11 different kinds.

Lady's bedstraw, or more accurately Our Lady's bedstraw, was so called because it was believed, according to a medieval legend, that the Virgin Mary lay on a bed of bedstraw at the inn in Bethlehem, because the donkeys had eaten all the other fodder in the stable. The fragrance of lady's bedstraw is honey-like and lingeringly lovely, and it can be detected many feet away.

The plant contains a chemical called coumarin which, when made into the drug dicoumarol, will prevent blood from clotting. But not only does the plant produce this powerful anti-coagulant, its flowers were also once used for curdling or coagulating milk into cheese and junkets. This pretty plant was also used in footbaths for refreshing tired feet.

The history behind our wild plants is a fascinating subject – for lady's bedstraw was at one time used for bedding material, because it was valued not only for its beauty but for its honey-like scent, the actual smell of new-mown hay being given off by the fine whorls of its leaves when dried, which was also effective against fleas.

At one time vinegar was made from the juices of lady's bedstraw, a yellow dye was extracted from its leaves and stems, and a red dye from its roots. The plant was also used to treat epilepsy and gout.

Old names for lady's bedstraw include cheese-rennet and cheese running, a-hundred-fold (there being so many flowers on the plant), curd-wort and bed-flower.

Sweet woodruff, so starry and prettily flowered, like lady's bedstraw, also contains coumarin and gives off the scent of hay, especially when dried. The whole of the Rubiaceae family is a very dainty and pretty one with characteristically cruciform flowers.

*11 July 1994*

Ladie's Bedstraw *Galium verum*

# MELANCHOLY BEAUTY

CHANGE and decay brings a melancholy beauty to autumn as green chlorophyll in leaf cells breaks down, leaving a glorious range of mellowing reds and yellows and golden-browns in the countryside around us.

Today, I went for a walk in a wood strewn with copper-coloured leaf-litter among which there were many yellowing sycamore leaves blotched with tar-spot fungus.

Broken pieces of chestnut lay scattered on the floor with spiny-jacketed nuts clustered to the twigs like little hedgehogs. The bark of the sweet chestnut tree was full of fissures and ridges with a slightly spiralling twist, and its many leaves were paling into yellow and deepening into gold.

I was surprised to discover foxgloves still in flower in the wood, their lingering, magenta spotted finger-bells, full of hidden beauty. My eyes settled for many moments on dying blackberry leaves – yellow ones veined with green, and green ones flushed with copper and rose, their fiery tints fused to perfection.

I passed a large female yew tree, its sombre foliage of needles decked with little fruits like pink cups fashioned from wax.

The canopy of the wood was fanned with traceries of twigs among its arching branches, with many of the tree trunks below thinly powdered with an emerald algal bloom. Near the edge of the wood, I discovered a dense patch of butcher's-broom which was stiff and spiny and green, with a few of its leafy branches bone-coloured and beautifully skeletonised.

Butcher's-broom, perhaps the strangest of all our native plants, was once gathered and bundled and sold to butchers for sweeping their chopping blocks. Along the boundary of the wood, I found several blue spikes of germander speedwell, and herb-robert still brightly in flower.

As I left the wood, I stopped to pick a few bluebells, their papery fruit capsules and long stems as brittle and bleached as straw. It was difficult to believe such spectres had ever been part of a green world with moments of great beauty in a misty blue twilight of little bells.

I walked home brooding over the withered state of the bluebells, the composure of my mind slightly disturbed, for every living thing, however perfect its creation, is so subject to mortality.

*24 October 1988*

# WILD ORCHIDS

WILD orchids are a fascination to me, especially those that fall into the spellbinding colour-range of rosy-purple, magenta, pinky-mauve, and lilac, with all their sensitive and beautiful shades and tints, so infinitely varied, that charm the eye.

Over the last three months, I have spent many magical moments with wild orchids – those I have discovered for myself, and others whose closely-guarded secrets I have been privileged to share.

Sometimes there have been so many – particularly marsh orchids and common spotted orchids – that putting one's feet down in their world became a charming little nightmare in mine. Recently the world has worn an excited little path to our cottage door telling me where bee orchids could be found, and I have visited charming groups – with velvety bumblebee lips and pinky-mauve sepals – growing at Wymondham, Silfield, Ashwellthorpe, Long Stratton and Fersfield.

Today, not far from the parish boundary of Ashwellthorpe, I have been revelling in yet another enchantment – the scented orchid, whose powerfully pretty fragrance surpasses any perfume or scent of any other flower I have ever known. The flowers have long puce-coloured spurs filled with clear nectar, which can only be reached by insects with long tongues, such as butterflies and moths.

There are about fifty different species of wild orchids growing in Britain, and I have looked at ten different kinds during the last three months, all growing wild in the area of Norfolk in which I live. Man orchids, a species I have always wanted to find, and probably never will, whose flowers bear a fanciful but striking resemblance to little men in big helmets, complete with arms and legs, were first recorded in Norfolk in 1785, growing in my own village Ashwellthorpe. They also used to grow in Bracon Ash, Bunwell, Forncett and Tacolneston. I often wonder if even one of these very rare native orchids is there to be discovered in any of these villages today. To me – just a peep at one would be worth a ransom.

*1 August 1987*

Fragrant Orchid *Gymnaolenia conopsea*

# MORNING GLORY IS A HEDGEROW HIGHLIGHT

*B*ELLBINE is beautiful at the moment, festooning hedgerows with snowy-white trumpets and heart-shaped leaves. I often pause on my walks to admire the luxuriant growth of this plant which climbs by twining round the stems and branches of other plants, always twisting in a counter-clockwise direction.

The flower-trumpets are big and eye-catching and at dusk they become almost luminous in the fading light. They are unscented both day and night.

Bellbine, my favourite name for the plant, often remains in place along a hedgerow or at the edges of woods for many years. So strong are the fibres in its stems it has acquired the name of rope-bind.

The flower-trumpets contain very long stamens in the middle of which there is a tall white stigma and style. Nectar is secreted at the base of the flower. The fruit is a globular capsule, the seeds dark brown.

The flower-trumpets on a few stems which I collected from a hedgerow for tests stayed unfurled and wide open all night. Some observers of the plant report that the trumpets stay fully open on moonlit nights, but close on dark nights. Other names for this plant are old man's nightcap and great withywind.

Bellbine is in flower from July to September. It belongs to the *Convolvulaceae* family which includes the charming little field bindweed with sprawling pink and white trumpets which can often be seen trailing along the edge of the roadside, also sea bindweed of coastal sands with pretty pink or pale purple trumpets.

How important hedgerows are as a framework for climbing plants. For they give support not only to bellbine, but also to hops and honeysuckle, black bryony and white bryony, and to traveller's-joy too.

No wonder bellbine is also known as morning glory, for these big snowy-white trumpets are indeed the glory of the hedgerows at the moment.

*7 September 1998*

Greater Bindweed *Calystegia sepium*

# ACORNS BY THE TON

INSIDE every acorn there is an oak tree! How I love to ponder over these profound words, for it puts the miracle of life into such an awesome perspective.

The acorn harvest this year is phenomenal – verges, pavements, roads and gutters are littered with numerous acorns and what is so appealing is the way it fits so snugly into its cup.

English acorns I picked up today to examine with a hand lens proved to be more beautiful than I had realised.

In fact the cup, so finely fashioned, was infinitely more beautiful than the acorn itself.

The English oak, also known as the common oak or pedunculate oak, is one of two oaks native to Britain, the other oak being the sessile oak or durmast oak, whose acorns "sit" on the twigs.

Reaching about a 100 feet and taking up to a 100 years to mature, the English oak may live for 800 years or more, producing its first acorns at about 60 years of age.

By the reign of Queen Elizabeth I, English oaks, because of their great strength and durability, had become used so extensively for building ships and timber-framed houses, that legislation had to be passed to protect the tree, which was followed by replanting in royal forests.

Acorns, which are really large oval nuts, were at one time of prime importance for feeding pigs turned loose in the forests in the autumn.

Right of pannage, as it was called, exists to this day, the word pannage deriving from the Norman French pesner, meaning to grub out with the snout.

Acorns are welcome food for mice and squirrels, wood pigeons, pheasants and woodpeckers; forgotten acorns buried by jays becoming oaks!

Oaks, which live longer than all our other native trees, have had many uses including the provision of timber for hammer-beams, rood-screens, pews and pulpits; refectory tables, chairs, chests, benches, stools and cupboards; and flooring, panelling and staircases; even the roots of the oak have been used for making knife handles.

The oak is a remarkable tree. It is an interesting thought that there are more than 450 different species of oak growing in this world.

*14 October 1995*

English oak acorns *Quercus robur*

# Winter

*Heigh ho! sing heigh ho! unto the green holly:*
*Most friendship is feigning, most loving mere folly:*
*Then, heigh ho! the holly!*
*This life is most jolly*

                As you like it
                Act 2nd. Scene 7th.

# PLENTY OF CLUES FOR WOODLAND DETECTIVES

$\mathcal{D}$ROPPINGS can provide interesting information about wild animals and their way of life, and so can food pellets containing indigestible material, such as those regurgitated by owls. Also animal paths or runs, and tracks made by cloven hooves; as well as feeding signs such as empty cherry stones, gnawings and nutshells – all of them fascinating clues as to who is living where, and eating what or whom.

Detective work in a wood can be not only engrossing but highly instructive.

Recently Peter Aspinall of Stoke Holy Cross and I went searching for signs in a wood in South Norfolk. We discovered fox droppings of a kind neither of us had ever seen before. On breaking them open we found they consisted of a mass of grey, half-digested chippings from sugar beet, some of which were piled in a field not far from the wood.

Fox droppings, tapered at both ends and with a very characteristic tail, are easy to identify. They always bring out the detective in me, for sadly they often contain recognisable remains of prey such as small bones and fur. Other fox droppings we found contained a mass of bullace stones, and some discovered by Peter were full of rose hips.

We noticed many cloven hooves, small ones and big ones – the tracks of red deer – had passed before us on our pathway. We looked at their droppings which consisted of many large black pellets loosely clumped together, their surfaces ribbed or furrowed. We also looked at a muddy wallow made by the deer.

Rabbits, who use their faeces for scent-marking their territories, often defecate on elevations such as mole hills. We noticed that a sawn tree stump had been used as a depository for many rabbit droppings. Nearby there was another sawn tree stump, this time a squirrel's picnic table scattered with hazelnut shells, opened in halves. We were amused how the tree stumps had become used for such different purposes, neither being misused for the other.

We noticed that bunches of leaves on the woodland floor had been drawn into worm burrows, and that pheasants had been digging up ramson bulbs. We crushed some of those which were scattered about, the smell reminding us of cloves of garlic.

What an interesting time we had had in the wood examining all the evidence, interpreting and establishing the facts. We had not encountered a single deer, fox, rabbit, pheasant or squirrel. But we knew they were there all right, by the evidence each had left behind. And doubtless some of them were busy observing us, unobserved!

*30 December 1990*

# SMALL COPPERS FIND THEIR WAY

Yesterday I walked round the meadow at the back of our cottage, which had been cut for hay in July. A few creeping thistles, mown down at the same time, had re-grown – only a foot high, freshly green and spiny, they were in flower, all over again.

My attention as I approached them became riveted to their mauve crowns. For feasting on the nectar among the honey-scented florets were 19 small copper butterflies. The sight of so many coppery-orange butterflies on so few thistle heads, was sheer magic. The little mauve thistles were orange with wings, all of them open in the sunshine and just like dainty orange bows pinned to the thistle heads.

I was astonished to see, among all the small coppers, one with the palest of gold wings, that is, pale gold where the copper-coloured areas should be. It was in mint condition including its iridescent sheen.

I noticed all these burnished little butterflies closed their orange wings when a cloud obscured the sun, and opened them immediately the cloud had passed by. With no other plants in flower on the meadow, except a dog daisy here and there, how did 19 small coppers know this small amount of thistle nectar was in the corner of the meadow?

I returned to the meadow to film the butterflies which were so preoccupied with probing in the florets for thistle nectar after two hungry days of rain, that the lens of my video camera, only an inch or two away, caused them no disturbance whatsoever. These vivid, small copper butterflies, so dainty and lustrous, belong to the same family as the beautiful little blues and the hairstreaks, which include some with metallic sheen so iridescent that the butterflies have been described as "flying jewels."

The egg of the small copper, which resembles a tiny white golf ball, is laid singly on the leaves of common sorrel or sheep's sorrel, and occasionally on broad-leaved docks – but, only when the sun is shining!

The larva, not conforming at all to the traditional image of a caterpillar, is shaped rather like a woodlouse. There are usually two, sometimes three or very rarely, four (in the south), generations of small coppers in a year, depending on the summer weather.

My little colony on creeping thistles in October is third generation here in Norfolk, according to Michael Hall. I wonder where their food plants grow. I expect there is common sorrel in the wood nearby, or maybe I have missed it in the meadow.

*7 October 1994*

# DELIGHTFUL RAMBLE DOWN BY THE RIVER

*I* love rambling along riversides among water-loving plants, enjoying the peacefulness and serenity of a river going by, and occasional chats with its anglers.

Water life is fascinating. One of my favourite idling places is along a winding stretch of the River Yare where carp, roach, dace and bream live, along with gudgeon, pike, rudd, tench and perch.

Yesterday, while wandering beside this beautiful stretch of river, I stopped to watch an engaging little scene of 11 mallard, their floating reflections and those of the overhanging willows stippled in the surface. I passed many common reeds, our tallest native grass, their shaggy heads and narrow leaves all characteristically leaning the same way.

Wild angelica was still in flower, its white umbels soft to the touch and faintly flushed with pink. The call of a waterhen – a strident metallic "krrrrk krrrrk" – betrayed its presence among the water plants nearby. The alders overhanging the Yare were hung with corky cones, their red catkins tightly bunched, ready for release next spring. I stopped to listen to the patter of poplar leaves as the wind combed through the trees.

There were many riverside patches of white dead-nettle, their stems whorled with snowy-white flowers. An angler, fishing for chub, informed me that although there were many fish in the river, some had ulcers and were in poor condition.

Gipsywort whorled with nutlets, and seeding water figwort, overhung the banks of the river. Where the river widened and became more shallow there was a luxuriant stretch of water forget-me-nots, their enamel-blue flowers and pink buds resting on the surface of the water.

Further along I paused to talk to another angler who was fishing for gudgeon with maggots, the gudgeon being used as bait for pike. Gudgeon, were considered such a delicacy last century that they were given to invalids to eat.

During my walk I stopped for many moments here and there along the banks to watch the river going by... always going by, day after day, century after century. White water in sunny shallows swiftly furling over stony beds... deep water round bends, glassy and full of reflections... surfaces shot with broken lights... surfaces beaten like pewter.

The voice of the river, silent where deep, or gurgling and plopping over pebbles where shallow. The voice of the wind hissing through the reeds, or soughing through the alders and willows. Peacefulness, tranquillity... solitude and serenity... water for ever going by...

*6 November 1996*

# BEAUTIFUL WAYSIDE FLOWER

WHEN we were children we used to delight in opening and closing the mouths of the snapdragons in the flower-beds by squeezing their throats. One can do exactly the same thing with common toadflax, whose flowers of primrose and orange look like tiny garden snapdragons.

To me, the diminutive toadflax sprinkled along the verges of late summer and autumn is far more beautiful than the antirrhinum of the flower-beds. Common toadflax, which I have beside me as I write, is a perennial with a creeping rhizome which produces tall stems with leaves that are grass-like, spirally arranged and of a sea-green hue.

The stems are clustered with slender corollas of yellow, most attractively lipped on their lower lobes with bright orange, at the back of which there is a golden throat thickly ridged with hairs. The flowers taper into yellow spurs which are long, hollow and pointed with nectar in their tips which attracts pollinating bees with long tongues.

The fruit is plump and oval and if you open one of them you will find the capsule crowded with seeds which are flattened and blackened, each one encircled by a wing.

The flowers of the toadflax were at one time steeped in milk and placed on tables in farmhouses to attract and destroy flies. Infusions were also made from the leaves of the toadflax, which were added to water drunk by poultry to cure "drooping". The plant was also much used as a remedy for jaundice.

Over the centuries country folk have given toadflax a most imaginative collection of names which include butter-and-eggs and bunny-nose, lion's mouth, devil's head and weasel-snout, pattens-and-clogs, pig's chops and squeeze-jaw, the last name being particularly apt. Toadflax belongs to the figwort family which includes foxgloves and speedwell, brooklime and eyebright.

A curious condition known as peloria sometimes occurs in toadflax whereby the corolla becomes regular with five spurs.

Foxgloves and Canterbury Bells are also subject to peloria, producing the most beautiful spotted, frilly flower-discs at the top of the flower-spike.

*5 November 1991*

Common Toadflax *Linaria vulgaris*

# BUTTERFLY IS BRILLIANTLY DISGUISED AS A DEAD LEAF

*A* few days ago, for a brief magical moment, I stood in the sun beside a bramble patch watching a comma butterfly sipping juices from an overripe blackberry. Its tongue, like a watch-spring fully uncurled, was probing among the many drupelets which formed the fruit of the blackberry.

The butterfly suddenly closed its fiery-orange wings and became a "dead brown leaf", withered in outline and upright, and with a distinctive white comma on the lower part of the "leaf", a "leaf" so dead, in fact, among the brambles it became indiscernible.

After a few moments, the "dead leaf" began to open, revealing fiery-orange wings again. The butterfly basked on the brambles in the sunshine, and after further probes for blackberry juice closed its colourful wings and became a dead brown leaf again… which suddenly flew away!

Marvelling at the incredible design of the butterfly, I turned away from the bramble patch thinking if only I could have journeyed down a slightly different evolutionary pathway, one, in fact, with the resplendency of wings!

Several rainy days have passed by since my brief encounter with the comma butterfly which will now have gone into hibernation in the wood behind our cottage. There it will rest on a branch or tree trunk, its withered leaf look protecting it to the point of being invisible as a butterfly.

No other butterfly in Britain is remotely similar to the comma which has a raggedly beautiful symmetry which is quite unmistakable. Its eggs are fluted and glassy-green and laid singly on nettles, elm, sallow or hop.

The caterpillar lives beneath, then later on top of, the leaf, and it is camouflaged as a bird-dropping! The chrysalis, which is marked with silver, coppery-gold and an opaline iridescence, hangs like a seahorse upside down.

Nineteenth century textbooks give hops as the principal food plant of the comma but as commercially grown hops declined during the last century, the burning of the vines and more effective treatment of the hops all contributed to this butterfly's increasing rarity.

Today the comma is once again widely distributed and locally common in wooded areas. Its 20th century change from hops to the common nettle as its primary food plant appears to have been the main reason for its recovery.

To be camouflaged as a bird-dropping while a caterpillar, and disguised as a dead leaf while a butterfly is truly remarkable – both of them masterpieces of natural deception.

*4 November 1996*

# MAGICAL COLOURS

$\mathcal{M}$ANY times during the summer and autumn I have stopped to look at field scabious and devil's-bit scabious; field scabious is an amethyst pin-cushion of stamens, and devil's bit, a domed button of violet.

I have watched small copper butterflies of burnished orange on the purple heads of the devil's-bit, a little scene which is delicately beautiful in a magical clash of colour.

The devil's-bit scabious adorns Flordon Common, its numerous tubular florets pollinated by butterflies and bees. The root of the devil's-bit terminates rather abruptly, "the Devil having bitten part of it away, enviously, to put an end to the plant's good works of curing many ailments; the shortened root, however, having failed to destroy the devil's-bit curative properties".

Misty mauve heads of field scabious, even at this time of the year, can still be found along the verges, like neatly frilled pin-cushions, the stamens giving the impression of the pins, and the little mauve florets, the pin-cushion.

On close inspection the pin-like stamens can be seen to bear anthers set see-saw fashion on the ends of their filaments, which move at the slightest little touch. One of the delights of the field scabious is the subtle variation in its spectrum of mauves which, delicate and charming, range from the softest of lilacs to amethyst. A rounded green head, bristling with seed cases, replaces the flower which is nearly as beautiful as the scabious flower itself.

The field scabious acquired its name from the reputation its juice once had for curing the disease scabies, drunk in an infusion or applied in the form of an ointment. Scabious is known by several other names including lady's pin-cushion and pins-and-needles, also bachelor's buttons, which is shared by other flowers.

Field scabious has a delicate honeyed scent attracting butterflies and bees.

This summer I have watched many a small tortoiseshell butterfly visiting field scabious, and how beautiful they are with wings of orange, beaded with blue, alighting on a flowerhead of amethyst.

*6 November 1991*

Field Scabious *Knautia arvensis*

# FEATHERED BALLET

A few days ago while driving through Saxthorpe I stopped to watch a "feathered ballet" in a wayside field. The more I looked, the more absorbing it became, the eye drawn along by the tractor, the plough, and its cloud of wheeling wings.

The tractor tilted in its furrow moved up and down the field, the driver, lifting and reversing his five-furrow plough in a sweep of twinkling wings.

The gulls waited in rows across the field for the tractor's return, and when the wheels were perilously near, they rose into the air in a cloud of arched wings wheeling round the back of the tractor where they settled in a clamorous wrangle on the newly-turned worms.

Lapwings, whose winter home is so often the arable field, were also present at the feast; but these graceful birds with their iridescent pied plumage were mobbed by the gulls, and they hung about a little to one side, ceaselessly driven away from the tantalising feast.

The rhythm of the ploughing and feasting with the ever-rolling blizzard of birds was mesmerising to watch, and one wondered from time to time about the tractor driver alone with his thoughts, insulated in his cab from this world of wild wings.

As I drove home leaving this picturesque scene behind me, I was amazed to discover not half a mile away another tractor tilted in its furrow ploughing up and down another field. But strange to say, the tractor driver and the earthworms had the newly-turned soil all to themselves.

Yesterday while on my way to Holt I stopped to look at the field which I had watched with such rapt absorption. It was bare and brown and empty with such a stillness in the air. But memory lingers strangely on, for that blizzard of wings remained twinkling in the mind long after they had gone.

*8 February 1989*

# MYSTERIOUS WORLD INSIDE A DELIGHTFUL 'PINCUSHION'

*R*OBIN'S pincushions are exceptionally beautiful though neither robin nor pincushion, they are one of nature's strangest delights. Large, mossy and ball-shaped, they are to be found in hedgerows on the stems of both the dog rose, and the field rose.

These red and green bedeguars, as they are also called, are the larval homes of a tiny parasite gall wasp called *Diplolepsis rosae*. When I was a child I used to delight in finding these balls of coloured threads, quite unaware that they were abnormal growths of rose tissue and were, in fact, nature's strange and beautiful reaction to the mischief wrought by a tiny female wasp.

It was many years before curiosity overcame my wonder at the beauty of the robin's pincushion, and I actually dared to ruin one of them by cutting it open with a kitchen knife. What I found there astonished me for the ball was filled with cells each containing a tiny white larva.

The little gall wasp lays here eggs in spring in the young leaf buds of the rose. When the larvae hatch, the mossy ball begins to develop round them. It can have as many as 60 chambers, each occupied by a baby gall wasp larva. Here they feed, over-winter and pupate, producing adults the following May.

The mossy balls, or galls, which are fully formed by July, were are one time collected form the hedgerows and ground into a powder for the treatment of colic and kidney stones. The galls were also used to make bedeguar tea which was used to cure diarrhoea in cattle.

What is unbelievable is that this mysterious world inside the mossy ball is sometimes occupied by other parasites who, in turn, are liable to attack by hyperparasites; thus an amazing community of fascinating complexity develops – the primary parasite, the secondary parasites, and the hyperparasites.

There can also be lodgers whose larvae may be devoured by a chalcid wasp. One cannot but marvel at the relationship between the dog rose and the robin's pincushion and the odd little world within it. For it is not only beautiful, but balanced, that is, not causing mortal damage to the dog rose.

*7 December 1996*

Robin's pincushion Home of *Diploepsis rosae*

# CHURCHYARD LICHENS

THERE is a little world about us of lowly plants with long Latin names and no flowers, and they live on roofs and chimneys, trees and fences, walls, sills and lintels.

Some of them almost clothe tombstones, and even live on milestones, and others find a humble home beneath the posh plants in flower-pots.

Some of them live velvety lives, some crusty lives, and others leafy, tufty lives, and all of them though everywhere about us live little lives beyond the bounds of very much human attention.

They grow in patches, and in cushions, and they creep about in little carpets, and sometimes we tower above them treading on them.

If we bent down and really looked at them, it is just possible we might learn to love them, and even be a little thoughtful towards them, for mosses, lichens and liverworts are plants just as beautiful in their way, as those we all know which bear flowers.

Over the past fortnight I have visited many village churchyards in Norfolk where there is a fascinating wealth of centuries-old stone. With a powerful lens I have examined many medieval nooks and crannies and church surfaces, which must have been colonised for centuries by lichens and mosses.

And on the south side of the churches I have looked at 18th and 19th century tombstones, whose weathered surfaces were often a riveting mosaic of pretty lichens in delicate bluish-greens, snowy-greys, and crusty little sunsets of orange with cinnamon touches.

Some of the plants formed flat ragged rosettes, others granular patches often growing among cushions of silvery-green moss.

I found weighty ledger slabs that had vanished under plushy gardens of mosses, and table tombs encrusted with lichens.

I love "poking about" in village churchyards, and in the chilly December damp I had a most absorbing time scrutinising the tiny intricacies of these flowerless little plants living on the gravestones.

The lichen flora of our churchyards is an ignored part of our wildlife heritage, and the clearance of headstones from their original sites is not only vandalising village history, and breaking faith with those who lamentingly put them there, but it removes the most fascinating of lichen records as well.

*18 December 1987*

# HARVEST OF THE HEDGEROWS

*B*ERRIES are beautiful and a delight to the eye, brightening the hedgerows at this time of the year. How I love the harvest of the hedgerows with its colourful wild tints – so important a food source for a variety of birds as well as bank voles and wood mice.

One hundred and ninety thousand miles of hedgerow have been destroyed in this country since the second world war, and those that are left are often flailed of their fruits and berries, or so vestigial that they become boundary markers of little use for wildlife.

I spend part of every day walking along the lanes in the parishes among which I live.

Much of the time is spent examining hedgerows. Those trimmed every second or third year are not only the most attractive but the most prodigious where the fruit and berry harvest is concerned.

There are few plants more beautiful at this time of the year than the arching spray of a dog rose wandering astray in an untrimmed hedgerow, scattered with scarlet hips like fairy light bulbs – or the red haze of countless haws ripening through ever-deepening shades of crimson.

The beauty of black bryony garland twisted through a hedgerow has riveted my eye on several occasions just recently – their red and green and orange berries like coloured beads threaded on a vine. Dogwood with its red twigs and rounded black fruits is a feature of many of our hedgerows at the moment, its oval leaves undergoing pretty colour-changes from green to a soft tint of pinkish-red. Female hollies in the hedgerows are already looking Christmassy and woody nightshade is glistening with berries in clusters of ruby drops.

Yesterday I brought home from my walk a splendid, scarlet cluster of flask-shaped hips picked from a sweet briar – a wild rose easy to identify because of the tantalising smell of fresh apples released from glands when the leaves are bruised between the fingers.

Today I brought home spindle fruits already sealing-wax pink. I could not resist opening one of these intriguing pink fruits to peep inside its orange-coated seeds.

Hedgerows should be cherished not only for their beauty and the species they contain, but particularly for the food they provide for our berry-eating birds.

*8 October 1994*

Dog Rose Hips *Rosa canina*

# GOOD TIMES WITH OLD FRIENDS

Our cottage is called "Red Squirrels" in remembrance of the happiest days of my natural history life.

The latest *Norfolk Bird and Mammal Report* arrived on my desk a few days ago. On the outside of the cover there is a beautiful photograph of a red squirrel with long ear tufts, a blonde tip to its tail, and shoe-button eyes.

The squirrel is gazing directly into the eyes of those looking at it. Inside the book it states – "Sadly, the red squirrel is now confined to Thetford Forest where a small remnant population remains." Underneath are the dismal words "no records."

To me the red squirrel is the most charming of all the creatures ever to have evolved on this planet. Its appeal lies in the characteristic pose of the paws folded across the chest, the most beautiful of all tails in the animal kingdom – curved against the spine, like a brush, fur the colour of a fox.

The sadness I felt on looking at the squirrel on the cover of the report resonated through me, stirring memories of pain, and joy, for I was once a trusted "member" of a group of eight red squirrels.

In 1962 I visited Ashwellthorpe for the first time to view the house we still live in today. It consisted of timber-framed and clay lump cottages joined together. To my astonishment, while examining the back of the cottages, a red squirrel ran along the roof gutter.

Riveted by the squirrel… I bought the cottages! The squirrels, who lived in the 93 acres of deciduous woodland behind the cottage, became part of the everyday life of the cottage itself.

I bought vast quantities of hazel nuts, like sacks of coal, to feed eight squirrels obsessed with nuts. I used to scour Norwich market and local shops as supplies seasonally dwindled, hoarding any nuts I could find, fearful that they would run out.

The squirrels were fed through an open window in the kitchen, their claws clasped around my fingers as they took the nuts out of my hand. The dextrous handling, rotating and opening of the nuts, was fascinating to watch, empty hazel nuts unerringly discarded without ever opening and checking their contents. I used to gather them up and open them myself.

There was never anything worth eating inside them. The squirrels soon acquired names. The most loved of them was Hognut, a dominant female, who used to sit on the lawn hogging a pile of nuts. Swivelling round while flashing her tail in anger, she would face competing squirrels taking runs at her nuts.

These included Torn-Ear, Bare-Patch, Long-Legs senior and Long-Legs junior, their hind legs being noticeably longer than those of the other squirrels.

Such was their passion for nuts, they used to arrive at the cottage at dawn to eat those put out ready for them last thing at night. When the nuts had all been eaten, they ran up the roof and climbed down the chimneys into the cottage itself to look for more nuts, their red fur blackened with soot.

The "black" squirrels used to sit on the window sill in the kitchen looking through the glass at the red ones sitting on the ledge the other side. Soot was pattered and smeared and sprinkled everywhere – a local builder eventually wiring over the chimney tops for me.

Then, disaster struck of a terrible kind. As I fed the squirrels by hand sitting on a stool in the garden I began to notice watering eyes, then swollen and discharging noses, then eyes that were almost blind confining the squirrels to the ground.

One by one they died. And one by one they were buried in the garden. The heartbreak will never really leave me, nor the pain in the mind. Long-Legs senior was sent to the laboratory for examination. He had died of a virus similar to that of myxomatosis. I can still feel their claws clasped round my fingers.

I can still see Hognut defending her nuts, angrily facing the other squirrels and stamping her feet as she swivelled round to scold them. Those days will never return, because there can never be another Hognut.

*12 April 1997*

Red Squirrel *Sciurus vulgaris*

# SPARHAM POOLS

*I* went to Lyng a few days ago, the old part of which is sylvan and beautiful, with the River Wensum pouring through a row of old arches underneath a red brick bridge.

Near this picturesque corner of Norfolk, there is a turning to Sparham pools, where there are about 30 acres of beautifully healed and flooded gravel workings.

Gorse and broom fringe the pools, as well as birch and willow, and there are benches, well placed, for enjoying the tranquil scene across the water.

From the first seat, I watched several great crested grebes – handsome fishing birds – who last century, were almost exterminated because of fickle fashion demands for grebe feather hats.

I walked along a narrow path through shoulder-high broom, where I discovered another seat, from which I watched coot diving and disappearing under ever-widening circles of water ripples, and bobbing up again some 10 seconds later, their bills trailing with strands of green weed.

Reflected in the water at the far side of the pools were bracken and trees, in a shimmer of burnished auburn. Every so often the beautiful still silence of Sparham Pools was broken by the urgent, quacking descent of ducks' voices.

I stopped to watch mallard standing along the edge of an island – the drakes, handsome with their glossy green heads, butter-coloured bills, and orange feet.

I continued on my way round the perimeter of the pools, passing rose sprays sprinkled with fiery hips, a group of scaly toadstools like shaggy parasols, and lichen, its crusty surface crowded with long-stemmed cups.

There is a melancholy beauty about autumn's change and decay – its deep golden browns – and its copper-coloured leaf-litter under one's passing feet.

I climbed through the tree-tops of several leafy giants, toppled across my pathway by the recent hurricane.

I finished my walk looking at bramble leaves, some of them smarting with fiery tints and colour flushes, others, green, and prettily blotched and spotted with a crimson-staining rust fungus.

I left Sparham pools and Lyng, threading my way through several little lanes, with grasses and mosses growing down the middle of the tarmac, where I surprised a sinuous little animal with a black-tipped tail arching its way across some rough grass.

Nature is full of little scenes of predatory violence we rarely see – for the fortunate stoat was carrying a most unfortunate vole.

*20 November 1987*

# CLASH OF COLOURS IS AN ANNUAL DELIGHT

THE spindle tree is one of nature's treasures especially in the autumn when its fruits and leaves become so eye-catching and colourful. At the back of our cottage there is a very old hedgerow on one side of a meadow. Spaced along it are ancient pollarded oaks, some of such enormous girths their origins probably lie in Plantagenet acorns.

In between the oaks the hedge contains blackthorn and bullaces, dog roses and field roses, hazel, hawthorn, field maples and dogwood.

And here and there along the hedgerow there are spindle trees which at the moment are showered with bright pink fruits like little lanterns glowing with orange seeds. Their conflict of colours – bright pink and orange – fused perfectly together, make the fruits very beautiful.

Spindle a deciduous shrub, or small tree, of chalky soils, is a native of Norfolk's woods and hedgerows. For most of the year it is inconspicuous in the countryside, therefore easily overlooked, in fact rarely recognised.

But in the autumn the tree declares its identity with fiery pink leaves and colourful fruits which give it a coral-pink splendour, unlike any other of our native shrubs and trees.

Even its flowers in May and June pass unnoticed, for they are greenish-white and small, becoming visually lost among the leaves on the tree.

The old name spindle is a clear indication of the use to which the tree was once put. Long before the spinning-wheel was invented, woollen thread for weaving was wound on to spindles made from twigs cut from the spindle tree. And "spinsters", usually unmarried girls, rotated the raw wool on to the spindle.

Clothes pegs, small tools used by watch and clock makers, knitting needles, meat skewers, and pegs used by shoemakers, were all at one time made from the tough, hard wood of the spindle tree.

In medieval times the handsome pink fruits were dried and ground into a powder which was used for ridding children of head lice.

No native fruits are more beautiful than those of the the brightly-tinted spindle. How I look forward to their colour-clash, quaintness and charm, year after year.

*8 November 1997*

Spindle *Euonymus europaeus*

# THE UNTOUCHABLES

Stinging nettles – the untouchables of the plant world – are shunned by everybody, and my real interest in them only started when I discovered that they were dioecious.

Through years of conditioning I had not taken them very seriously, except as a food plant for certain caterpillars, and like everybody else – for avoidance purposes. Stinging nettles had no beauty, no presence like that of wild roses, and no fragrance like that of honeysuckle.

Then I discovered something interesting, that, unlike honeysuckle and wild roses, stinging nettle sexes were on different plants (doecious). There were male stinging nettle plants, and female stinging nettle plants quite separate in the same nettle beds.

Then I discovered something else which was even more interesting, and which finally reversed my attitude to stinging nettles for ever – that nettle fabric made from the fibres of stinging nettles was in use in Britain until last century for bedlinen, and what was even more remarkable that Bronze Age bones had been found wrapped in fabric made from nettle stems.

With all this riveting information very much in mind, I decided stinging nettles needed rethinking, and I started "browsing" in nettle beds where I noticed, much to my surprise, that stinging nettle flowers were even pretty.

The female plants bore long slender deep green catkins with minute white plumes, while the male plants bore prettily raised trusses crowded with pinkish-green buds.

While standing in the sunshine looking at nettle-beds in Saxlingham Nethergate, I noticed that puff after puff of pollen was leaving the male flowers in little explosions, dispersed within seconds. I discovered under magnification that the stamens which were bent inwards inside the buds, shot out as if on little springs, straightening themselves and flicking masses of pollen into the air.

I love looking at he way this world is created and discovering how it works, and my summer-long study of stinging nettles has been such a revelation, that they now have a proper place in my love of wild things.

Flowers, whether primroses or violets, bluebells or cowslips, are miracles of petals for all so see, but stinging nettle stamens flicking pollen-puffs "at the ladies" are scene-stealers we never see.

*15 December 1987*

# NATURE'S COLOURFUL NECKLACES ARE A JOY

$\mathcal{E}$VERY year during autumn's "season of mists and mellow fruitfulness" I revel in the beauty of the ripening berries of the black bryony as Nature adorns the hedgerows with her handiwork.

The magic of black bryony pursued me through my childhood. Its berries, bright and wild and beautiful, haunt me to this day. There was even a time when I used to decorate the brass lectern in Ashwellthorpe church at harvest time with these twining stems of colourful berries.

Black bryony is a member of the yam family. It is our sole native representative of a great tropical plant family.

It is not at all obvious why this plant should be called black bryony – its name actually arising from the colour of its fleshy, underground tuberous root, which in the Middle Ages was used internally as an emetic or purgative.

This climbing plant of the hedgerows always twines clockwise. Its many handsome leaves are glossy green, pointed and heart-shaped and they wreathe through the hedgerows in luxuriant trails on flexible stems.

Black bryony's summer climb through the hedgerows comes into its glory in the autumn when its clusters of green berries begin the most beautiful of colour-changes from green to yellow to orange to red – like shining coloured beads threaded on a vine. They spread picturesquely through the hedgerows like necklaces, or gay garlands, of eye-catching colour.

These beautiful berries are brilliantly enhanced as the leaves shrivel and finally perish to a fawnish-brown leaving Nature's necklaces of coloured beads fully exposed to view.

Black bryony has other names including snakeberry, beadbine – which is rather pretty – and blackeye root. Although the berries are poisonous, at one time they were collected in the autumn and preserved in gin or brandy to be used as a remedy for chilblains.

*3 December 1998*

Black Bryony *Tamus communis*

# FURRY CATERPILLARS

REARING caterpillars has been a lifelong love of mine, ever since "cabbage whites" and "woolly bears" kept in frilly-topped jam jars captured my imagination as a very small child. Those caterpillars, along with their food plants, and many other small creatures lent a magic to the long hours of childhood.

Caterpillars are nibblers and munchers as everyone knows, accumulating food reserves to provide building materials for the adult moths and butterflies.

And what an adventure that journey really is, turning plants into living cells and tissues, and reassembling them into remarkable new structures forming winged insects, fuelled by nectar.

There are many different types of caterpillars to be found in Britain – smooth ones, hairy ones, horned, striped or spotted ones, tufted, velvety or spiny ones; some with a fearsome appearance such as those of the puss moth or lobster; others, masterpieces of natural deception, mimicking twigs even to the point of mimicking the buds as well.

I have long loved furry caterpillars – the "woolly bears" of the garden tiger moth, the white ermines and yellow-tails, the oak eggars, drinkers and tussocks.

Recently Connie Doy of Flordon gave me one of the most beautiful of all furry caterpillars, a "Persian pussy-cat of a caterpillar" called the sycamore dagger. She had found it on the floor of a farm trailer in which bales of straw had been carted from Forncett St Mary.

It was yellow, with long, exquisitely silky fur. The sides of the caterpillar were smothered with yellow hairs, and splayed along the entire length of its back were pointed pairs of hair tufts, eight of which contained bright orange hairs.

Down the centre of its back, deep among the hair tufts was a striking line of white, arrow-headed spots edged with black. The caterpillar was 1½ inches long, and when handled it curled up into the most beautiful furry ring of pointed tufts – a starry coil of fluffiness weighing practically nothing.

The caterpillar was lively and when it eventually pupated I was very disappointed, because marvelling over its beauty had suddenly come to an end. The magic of caterpillars has pursued me all my life; and the transformation of a trundler on so many different legs – true legs, false legs and tail claspers – into a winged and beautiful insect is miraculous, perhaps even more so than man himself.

*9 October 1991*

# OLD MAN'S BEARD

Now is the time of year when old man's beard airily trails along the hedgerow in a curly grey smoke of plumed seeds. How well the plant's name expresses its massed fruits with their long feathery styles.

It is not often realised that this rather woody climber, whose stems can be as long as a hundred feet, is a member of the buttercup family.

The 16th century English botanist John Gerard, noticed that the plant "decked and adorned ways and hedges where people travel," so he called it traveller's joy, a name well-merited as it certainly claims the passer-by's attention.

The plant has some 40 other names including Virgin's bower and wild clematis, withywind and wild vine, old man, bindwith, hedge-rope and greybeard; also boy's bacca because the stems were at one time dried and smoked by boys.

It is rather surprising how often old man's beard is featured at its fruiting stage in English literature.

Gilbert White, on November 23 1788, noted in his journal "the downy seeds of traveller's joy filling the air." John Clare (1793-1864), in his Proposals for Building a Cottage, states: "Dig old man's beard from woodland hedge to twine a summer shade".

Tennyson likens "a vigorous old man firm upon his feet, to an oaken stock o'er-flourished with hoary clematis." Keats and Browning also wrote about old man's beard, both of them calling it Virgin's bower.

Curiously, the flowers of traveller's joy have no real petals, but have thick greenish sepals which curl back emphasising masses of pale yellow stamens. The leaf stalks are also curious for they serve as tendrils, twisting and twining in coiled springs to support the plant.

In the past the long woody stems of old man's beard were put to many uses including binding for farm gates and for keeping hurdles together. They were also used for weaving into bee-hives and rustic baskets.

The plant's plumed seeds arranged in light, feathery whorls are a wonder-world of beauty and design; for each seed is exquisitely endowed with a wavy tail of soft silky hairs to aid its future dispersal. These fluffy seeds wreathing along the hedgerows are white when new, but gradually turn smoky-coloured as wind and weather and dust soil them.

*28 November 1992*

# HOLLY WAS ROMAN INTRODUCTION

Of all the trees in the wood, the holly bears the crown – so go the lines of one of our oldest carols "The Holly and the Ivy", the holly with its pointed leaves and scarlet berries symbolising the crown of thorns.

Christmas and holly are inseparable. The twigs I have beside me as I write are strikingly beautiful, their berries brilliantly clustered among the prickliest of dark green leaves which shine as though varnished. Holly leaves have a leathery feel about them. The upper surface of the leaf is covered with a waxy, waterproof cuticle which protects it from excess water loss during the winter.

Holly has long been a symbol of Christmas. The monks of old called it the holy tree, to which holly probably owes its name, because they used it for decorating their churches.

The ritual use of holly originated in pre-Christian times. The Romans, who decorated their houses with evergreens, sent holly boughs to friends during the festival of the Saturnalia which coincided with the festival of the Nativity in Christian times. It is thought that early Christians gradually adopted Roman customs of using evergreens, including holly, for decoration. Early Christians who refrained from decorating houses with evergreen were persecuted by the Romans.

The berries contain four seeds, their angled faces fitting neatly together. Their pulpy flesh is an important source of winter food for birds including blackbirds, song thrushes and mistle thrushes, redwings and fieldfares, woodpigeons and collared doves, the seeds being dispersed in their droppings.

Nicholas Culpeper (1616–1654) herbalist, physician and apothecary wrote that holly berries were used to treat colic. They were also powdered for various medicinal uses including that of "binding the body." The itchy inflammation of chilblains was thrashed with holly "to let the bad blood out," and the bark of the holly was used in fomentations for broken bones.

Our ancestors had fascinating beliefs which I find most appealing. Holly was once planted near houses to keep away spells and enchantments. It was also pinned to bed curtains to keep away mischievous goblins!

*14 December 1990*

Common Holly *Ilex aquifolium*

# MISTLETOE – THE DRUID HEALER

Mistletoe has been associated with holly at this time of the year from time immemorial.

Nobody seems to know how or why it actually came to be associated so closely with Christmas at all. It is, however, known to have been connected with the pagan rites of the Druids of ancient Britain, the priests calling the plant "all heal" because they regarded it as sacred and a cure for every ill.

The Druids considered mistletoe to be particularly sacred when found growing on an oak tree, such reverence probably arising from the fact that it is so very seldom found growing there at all. In fact, legend has it that the Druids regarded mistletoe with such awe that their high priests could only gather it for use in their mystic rites by cutting it with a sickle made of gold.

Even during the Middle Ages it was still believed that mistletoe cured a wide range of ills, such as epilepsy, either by the sufferer eating the berries or wearing a sprig of it round the neck.

The best time to see mistletoe is in the winter when host trees have lost their leaves. In fact it is at this time of year that I love making lists of host trees, by mistletoe hunting in the tree-tops.

For example in Ashwellthorpe we have mistletoe anchored to apple and lime trees and frequently quite inaccessible except to birds, including the aptly-named mistle thrush which relishes such berries.

Mistletoe, a somewhat woody evergreen, growing mainly on the branches of deciduous trees, has been recorded on maple, lime, hazel, ash and poplar; willow, oak, pear and elm – its most common host being apple, particularly the crab.

Mistletoe grows very occasionally on evergreens and very rarely on conifers, neither of which have I ever seen.

But mistletoe is not just a magical plant for ritual kissing under its berries at Christmas. It also has a fiendish side to it which persists in certain European countries to this day, and that is the practice by trappers of catching and killing birds by the use of the glue from the mistletoe's seeds – a sticky birdlime – which is placed on the branches of trees which trap the feet of birds unfortunate enough to land on it.

When one really comes to think about it, it is quite extraordinary how one plant can have such a remarkable record of mystery, magic and superstition, probably arising from its strange parasitic nature, also being rooted, of course, so eerily above the earth.

*26 December 1994*

# USEFUL PLANT TO SCARE GOBLINS

*I*VY, or Hedera helix, is the only native member of the Araliaceae family in Britain. However, some authorities state that there are two native species which can be separated only by a microscope or high-powered hand lens when determining the starred shape of scale hairs on the plants.

Beautifully green, when all around in winter is skeletally bare, ivy's berry clusters are now swelling in the hedgerows and turning purplish-black.

There are many aspects which I love about ivy, one being the tiling effect of closely-set leaves on tree trunks, another being the pale green tracery of veins on the upper surface of the leaves and yet another, the umbels of scented, greenish-yellow flowers in September and October which produce the last great nectar feast of the year for small tortoiseshell butterflies, red admirals and painted ladies, as well as for moths and honey-bees and an assortment of flies, and for worker wasps for which it is the last food of their lives.

But not only do the insects feed on the nectar – nectar being important for the survival of queen wasps – they help with pollination too.

This produces rounded umbels of radiating berries for blackbirds and mistle thrushes, wood-pigeons, redwings, robins and song thrushes, and in April for newly-arrived blackcaps.

Ivy, because it was supposed to prevent intoxication, was dedicated to Bacchus, the Roman god of wine and was once a common sign on taverns. Hence the old proverb: "Good wine needs no bush," which also meant that good wine is undiluted, because a funnel made of ivy wood was supposed to have the power of separating wine and water.

In ancient Greek and Roman times ivy was used on ceremonial occasions to decorate the shields of warriors.

Ivy has long been a Christian symbol of everlasting life because its foliage is continuously green and it is a traditional part of the decorations at Christmas.

Yet another interesting reason for the use of ivy at this time of the year stems from the belief that house goblins were at their most malicious at Christmas-time, ivy at one time being hung on doors and over fire-places to guard against the mischief of the goblins.

*28 December 1994*

Ivy *Hedera helix*

# A BARN OWL SURVEYS ITS TERRITORY

*T*HE other day I was present at a scene which for a few precious moments dwindled the horrors of this world away.

I parked the car in a quiet little lane in Ashwellthorpe and, as I did so, a snowy-feathered barn owl came winging its way along the headlands and perched on a post beside the car.

For many moments it kept perfectly still; for many moments I kept perfectly still, my eyes never leaving this strikingly beautiful owl whose eyes were dark and rounded and forward-facing, in a large white face shaped like a heart.

After what seemed an eternity of suspense, the owl suddenly and silently left the post and flew just above the headlands along the field beside me in slow and deliberate long-winged flight movements, dipping and rising in its search for prey. It was one of those rare moments – I was present – the owl was present – we had both stopped for different reasons in the same place at the same time.

Daylight was just beginning to fail. The moon was shining in a blue sky flushed with rose. The horizon was a marvel of grey flooded with gold. The hedgerows were twiggy with tight little clusters of hazel catkins among arching sprays of rose hips, and along the verge there were many seeding heads of knapweed. Behind the hedge sheep were grazing and a cock pheasant was calling.

Time had stood so still for me, spellbound by the nearness and the beauty of the barn owl. It was only while dipping its snowy flight above the headlands that I had been able to see its biscuit-coloured back.

Vole-rich grassy headlands are so important to barn owls for hunting territories, also rough grassy verges, flailed no more than once a year.

Barn owls nest in farm buildings, church towers, disused and derelict buildings, lonely ruins, holes in old trees – even old nests.

Old barns were often built with a hole high up on an end wall which encouraged barn owls to nest inside, at the same time controlling the local population of mice. Modern barns can be adapted by cutting an access hole about eight inches square, and a large nest box can be placed high up in a dark corner. Once established as a breeding site the barn owls may well return year after year.

Although they are known to eat frogs and beetles, and even bats, their food consists chiefly of field voles, wood mice, common shrews and rats. Barn owls are also known as screech owls, a very apt name for their drawn out and eerie, rather chilling shrieks, which they make often when on the wing and while marking out their territory.

*30 December 1994*

# CHRISTMAS VIOLETS

THE grass was stiffly coated with frost this morning, and every leaf on the ground was exquisitely crystallised. The stinging nettles were granulated with frozen dew as though thickly sprinkled with a sugar sifter. Wherever I walked my boots crunched through the grass leaving deeply indented footprints, and fallen leaves were papery and noisy to tread on.

The sun from its low arc in the sky shone over the cottage roofs, bathing everything in a thin, pale light of chilly gold. The birds were hungry and under the boughs were many discarded spherical apple shells.

In the shelter of ivied elms and dog's mercury lay a bed of purple violets half-hidden from the eye among heart-shaped leaves. These diminutive flowers filled me with a strange stir of delight, for each with its tightly arched neck looked like a shepherd's crook bearing a flower with demurely laid-back petals.

I stood there for many spellbound moments for what magic there is in an unexpected discovery. The frost, which was everywhere else, had not reached the lee of the hedgerow. Each purple violet had a tiny lilac throat, and each heart-shaped leaf had a minutely scolloped edge. What an exquisite evolutionary partnership – purple violets and green hearts, each as beautifully designed as the other. There was no scent to the little carpet of violets spread out along the shoulder of the ditch, but within a half-hour of bringing a violet into the warmth of the cottage the scent was eye-shutting, as one breathed in its heady fragrance and exhaled a rapturous sigh.

Sweet violets, as these plants are called, are the only wild violets in Britain to have scented flowers. In days gone by they were strewn on the floors of cottages and churches to sweeten the damp or musty air. Their fragrance was also supposed to cure headaches and a syrup of sweet violets used to be given to children as a gentle purge. Even today oil is distilled from violet petals to make scent and flavouring.

How often memory lingers around childhood haunts, for these dear little purple flowers, so unobtrusive at one's feet, form a picture on the eye of the mind which is never forgotten. Violets – sweet violets – so purple, wild and appealing, have much to say to the listening heart.

*16 December 1986*

Sweet violet *Viola odorata*

# INDEX BY SUBJECT

(page numbers in **bold** type refer to illustrations)

**Animals**
banded snails, 54
bank voles, 73, 99, 102
bats, 12, 111
Daubenton's bat, 12
fox droppings, 90
frog, 30, 74, 111
grey squirrel, 60
harvest mice, 73
*Limax maximus*, 7, 12
long-eared bat, 1
lugworm, 77
mice, **73**, 88
pigs, 88
pink frogs, 30
rabbits, 90
rats, 111
red deer, 90
red squirrel, **101**
shrew, 73, 111
stoat, 102
tadpole, 74
wood mice, 111
worms, 16

**Birds**
avocet, 68
bird droppings, 94
bird-watching, 68
black-tailed godwits, 68
blackbird 3, 13, 79, 85, 94, 108, 110
blackcap, 110
collared dove, 108
coot, 102
cormorant, 68
curlew, 68
dawn chorus, 3
ducks, 102
dunlin, 68
fieldfare, 108
great crested grebe, 102
great-tit, 3
green sandpipers, 68
gulls, 96
jackdaw, 68
jay, 82, 88
lapwing, 96
mallard, 34, 60, 92, 102
marsh harrier, 65
mistle thrush, 108, 109, 110
moorhen, 5
nightingale, 38
owls, 28, 60, 90, 111
pheasants, 90
pigeons, 88
redwing, 108, 110
ringed dove, 60
ringed plover, 67, 68
robin, 3, 38, 110
rook, 3, 45
skylark, 66
snipe, 52, 68, 78
sparrow, 3

stone-runner, 67
thrush, 13, 38, 54, 108. 110
turtle dove, 28
warbler, 46
wood pigeon, 3, 13, 60, 108, 110
woodcock, 7
woodpecker, 88
wren, 7, 16, 29, 54
yellowhammer, 28

**Butterflies and Moths**
brimstone, 18, 62
burnished brass, 19
butterflies, general, 13, 62, 79, 86, 106
cabbage white, 106
caterpillars, 16, 94, 106
chrysalis, 94
clouded silver, 19
coma, 18, 94
common blue, 31
copper, 62, 91, 95
dark brocade, 19
death's head hawk, **19**
drinker, 106
elephant hawk, 19, 44
emerald, 19
emperor, 65
eyed hawk, 19
foxglove pug, 49
gate keeper, 62
hawk-moths, **19**, 44
herald, 12
holly blue, 32
light brocade, 19
little blue, 62, 91
lobster, **63**, 106
moths, general, 86, 106, 110
oak eggar, 106
orange-tip, 51, 32
painted lady, 68, 110
peach blossom, 19
peacock, 12, 18, 62
poplar, 19
privet hawk, 19, 44
pug, 19
puss, 19, 28, 106
rearing moths, 19
red admiral, 62, 110
ringlet, 62
rosy rustic, 19
scallop shell, 19
seraphim, 19
six-spotted burnet, 67
tortoiseshell, 18, 62, 95, 110
shuttle-shaped dart, 19
small white wave, 19
snout, 19
swallowtail, 65
sycamore dagger, 106
tiger, 106
V-pug, 19
wall, 32, 62

white admiral, 7
wood lady, 51
woolly bear caterpillar, 106
yellow tail, 106

**Ecological issues**
ditches, 75, 80, 112
ecological disaster, 50
essential habitats, 80
flail-cutters, 44, 50
hedgerows (see habitats)
verges, 24, 80, 88
verge-cutting, 37

**Fish**
bream, 91
carp, 71, 92
chub, 92
cockles, 77
dace, 70, 92
eels, 71
gudgeon, 70
minnow, 25
perch, 70, 92
pike, 70, 92
roach, 70, 92
rudd, 70, 92
ruff, 68
tench, 70, 92

**Flowers, plants and seeds**
aconite, 16, 10
acorn, 39, 82, **88**, 103
algal bloom 3, 20, 85
angelica, 78
antirrhinum, 93
beadbine, 105
bear's garlic, 58
bed-flower, 84
bee orchids, 86
belladonna, 46
bellbine, 50, 65, 70
bindweed, **87**, 67
bird's-foot trefoil, 28, 48, 67, 78, 81
black bryony, 28, 50, 64, 87, 99, **105**
blackberry, 79, 85, 94
blackthorn, 44, 50, 103
bladder campion, 80
bluebell, 7, 9, 26, **29**, 39, 60, 85, 104
bog bean, 52
bog pimpernel, 78
boy's bacca, 107
bracken, 102
bramble, 3, 9, 30, 64, 79, 94, 102
brandy bottle capsules, 48, 71, 84
brooklime, 30, 52
broom, 102
bugle, 22, 52, 55
bur chervil, 32

burnet rose, 43
butcher's broom, 85
buttercup, 29, 24, **35**, 52, 54, 55, 56, 78, 80, 107
canker rose, 43
catkins, 9
celandine, 7, 24, 29
centaury, common, 64
cleavers, 82
climbing fumitory, 46
coltsfoot, 10
comfrey, 70, 80
corn marigolds, 33
cow parsley, 29, **37**. 54, 80
cowslip, 21, **25**, 56, 104
creeping thistle, 91
cuckoo-buds, 56
cuckoo-pint, 7
cuckoo-spit, 72
daisy, common, **2**, 35, 56
dandelion clocks, 55, **83**
dandelion, 22, **40**, 83
dead-nettle, 92
devil's-bit scabious, 95
dog daisy, 9
dog rose hips, 99
dog rose, 28, 32, 42, 50, 54, 64, 81, 97, 99, 103
dog's mercury, 7, 12
dogwood, 28, 99, 103
Easter roses, 21
explosive mechanisms, 82
eyebright, 79, 93
fen-hay, 48
field maple, 54, 64, 82, 103
field penny-cress, 32, 33
field poppy, 28, 32, 81, 82
field rose, 28, 50, 97
field scabious, 18, 28, 54, **95**
figwort, 30, 93
fleabane, 68, 70, **75**, 78, 79
forget-me-nots, 32, 52
foxglove, 46, **49**, 60, 85, 93
fragrant orchid, **86**
frogwort, 35
fruits, 99
fumitory, 32
garlic mustard, 51
germander speedwell, 28, 32, 52, 85
gipsywort, 70, 92
gladden, 48
goat willow, 17
goat's-beard, 83
goose-grass, 82
gorse, 82, 102
great willowherb, 65, 75, 78, 79
ground-elder, 54
ground-ivy, 39, 54
hairy bittercress, 82
hare's-foot clover, 67
haws, 99
heartsease, 57

hedge woundwort, 46
hedge-parsley, 79, 80
hedgerow harvest, 50
hemlock, 32, 46
hemp agrimony, 46, 64, 79
herb robert, 29, 55, 85
hogweed, 3, 28, 54, **65**
holly, 60, 99
honeysuckle, 3, 7, 28, **44**, 48, 50, 64, 78, 81, 87, 103
hop, 94
ivy, 7, 13, 18, 60, 108, **110**
ivy-leaved toadflax, 47
Jack-by-the-hedge, 51
Jack-go-to-bed-at-noon, 28, 83
kingcup, 39, **52**, 57
knapweed, 18, 32, 111
lady's bedstraw, 67, **84**
lady's smock, 26, 51, 56, 57, 77
Love-in-idleness, 57
mallow, common, 81
man orchids, 86
marsh bedstraw, 78
marsh marigold, 24, 57
marsh orchid, 86
marsh pea, 65
marsh pennywort, 48, 71
marsh woundwort, 71
Mary-buds, 56
meadow vetchling, 28
meadowsweet, **31**, 48, 65, 75, 78, 103
mistletoe, 13, 109
morning glory, 87
moschatel, 29
mosses. 43, 54, 98, 102
nettles, 3, 104, 112
old man's beard, 50, 87, 107
ox-eye daisies, 28, 80
ox-slips, 56
parachute, 64, 83
pennywort, 78
pignut, 29
pilewort, 24,
pineapple weed, 32, 33
pink valerian, 46
plumed seeds, 107
primrose, 7, 9, 18, **21**, 25, 26, 45, 56, 104
purging buckthorn, 18
purple loosestrife, 18, 65, 70, 79
purple orchid, **7**, 26
purple salsify, 83
pussy willow, **17**
ragged-robin, 52, 78
ragwort, 64, 79
ramson, **58**, 90
red campion, 29, 32, 55, 80
red clover, 78
red poppy, **33**
reed, common, 65, 92

113

restharrow, 67
rose-hips, 13, 90, **99**, 102, 111
rosebay willowherb, **46**
rough chervil, 28, 42, 80
salsify, 83
samphire, 77
scarlet pimpernel, 32
sea bindweed, 67, 87
sea holly, 67
sea lavender, **77**
sea purslane, 77
sea rocket, 77
sea sandwort, 77
sea wormwood, 77
sedge, 48
seeds and seed dispersal, 40, 47, 51, 64, 82, 83
selfheal, 48, 78, 79
sheep's-bit 67
sneezewort, 78
snowdrop, **5**, 9, 14, **15, 20**
sorrel, common, 91
speedell, 29, 93
spleenwort, 12
spotted orchids, common, 86
stork-bill, 82
sweet briar, 42, 43, 99
sweet woodruff, 84
tansy, 25, 46, 65
teasel, 18
thistle, 18, 62
toadflax, **93**
trifid-bur marigold, 71
tufted vetch, 46, 65, 78
*umbellifors*, **85**
vetch, 54, 80
violets, 20, 21, 22, 26,45, 56, 104, **112**
viper's bugloss, 53
water figwort, 70
water forget-me-nots, **53**, 70, 92
water mint, 30, 52, 70, 75, 78
water soldiers, 48
water-crowfoot, 30
watercress, 30
white bluebell, 29
white bryony, 87
white campion, 28, 80.
wild angelica, 70, 92
wild radish, 33
wild rose, 42, 46, 104
wild thyme, 56
winter aconites, **20**, 24
winter heliotrope, 20
wood anemone, 6, 24, 26
yellow anemone, 6
yellow loosestrife, 65
yellow rattle, 52, 67, 78
yellow water lily, 48, 71, 82

## Folklore and Remedies
anti-coagulent, 84
bubonic plague, 35
chest complaints, 88
chilblains, 105, 108
colic, 97, 108
coughwort, 10
*coumarin*, 84
curdling, 84
*dicoumarol*, 84
*digitalin*, 49
dysentery, 75
emetic, 105
epilepsy, 84, 109
gentle purge, 112
goblins, 13. 108. 110
gout, 84
head lice, 103
headaches, 112
junket, 84
kidney stones, 97
magic, 109
natural insecticide, 75
nerve poison, 74
pannage, 88
pins-and-needles, 95
scabies, 95
superstition, 109
tired feet, 84
vinegar, 84

## Fungi
*Amanita phalloides*, 64
beef-steak fungus, 61
bird's nest fungus, 61
candle-snuff fungus, 61
*Coprinus comatus*, **61**.
*Coriolus versicolor*, 8, **26**
dead man's fingers fungus, 61
death cap fungus, 64
destroying angel fungus, 61
dryad's saddle fungus, 61
*Flammuline velutipes*, 26
ear-pick fungus, 61
earth-star fungus, 61
fungi, 8, 61
*Hypoxylon fuscum*, 26
Jew's ear fungus, 61
King Alfred's cakes, **8**
Lawyer's wigs fungus, 61
poison pie fungus, 61
scaly toadstools, 102
tar-spot fungus, 85

## Habitats
banks of streams, 75
banks, 80
boulder clay, 7
brackish marsh, 68
churchyards, 5, 12, 13, 20, 98
creeks, 77
ditches, 75, 80, 112
dykes, 48, 65
farmland, 66
fen, 48
freshwater marsh, 68
grassland, 66
gravel workings, 102
grazing marshes, 48
hedgerows, 17, 50 , 54, 78, 80, 87, 97, 99, 103, 105, 107, 110, 111
*hibernaculum*, 12
hollow oaks, 69
leaf canopy, 36
leaf-litter, 85, 102
marshland, 39, 46, 65, 68, 70, 71, 75
meadows, 66, 69, 70, 71, 78, 83
moors, 66
mudflats, 77
pastures, 78
ponds, 74
reed beds, 46, 48, 65, 68, 70, 71
riversides, 71, 75
roadsides, 83
Royal forests, 88
saltwater marsh, 68
sanctuary strips, 50
sand dunes, 66. 67
spring-fed bog, 52
tombstones, 98
tree stumps, 90
turf ponds, 48
verges, 24, 37, 80, 88
water butt, 74
wetlands, 48, 65, 75

## Insects and Beetles
bee-flies, 22
bees, 10, 13, 17, 35, 93, 107
beetles, 76, 111
Betty Beetle, 74
black longhorn beetle, 79
bumblebee, 22, 46, 49, 52, 54, 72, 80
burying betles, 76
caterpillar, 16, 94, 106
cave-spider, 12
chalcid wasp, 97
cocktail beetle, 16
damselflies, 32, 48, 54, 72
Devil's Coach Horse beetle, 16
earwigs, 16
fleas, 74
flies, 110
gall wasp, 43, 97
grave-digger beetle, 96
hornet, 13, **69**
hover-flies, 72, 79
humble-bee flies, 22
hyperparasites, 97
ichneumon fly, 63
larvae, 16. 63
ladybird, 26, 64, 70, 72
leaf coils, 54
leaf galls, 54
leaf-cutter bee, 41
leaf-rolling weevtls, 54
lesser Stag beetle, 16
mining bees, 22
mole flea, 75
nest-cells, 41
nymphs, 72
parasites, 63, 97
primrose sprite, 22
Robin's pincushion, 43, **97**
sexton beetle, 76
soldier beetles, 65
solitary bees, 22, 41
spiders, 16, 60
spittle-bug, 72
wasps, 13, 69, 70, 110
woodlouse, 7, 16, 91

## Other refs.
Anglo-Saxon, 58
Augustinian monks, 15
Bacchus, 110
Beatrix Potter, 4
Candlemas, 5, 14
Charles Darwin, 76
Christmas, 108, 109
Claude Monet, 33
Domesday Book, 19, 64
Druids, 109
E.A.E., 4
Early Christians, 108
Gavin Maxwell, 4
Izaak Walton, 25
Jeremy Bentham, 37
Linnaeus, 75
Medieval times, 103, 109
Nature Conservancy Council, 79
Queen Elizabeth, I, 31, 88
Raq, 4
Richeldis de Favarche, 14
Robin Goodfellow, 43
Romans, 5, 61, 75, 108, 110
Romany, 4
Samuel Pepys, 44
Shakespeare, 2, 25, 29, 36, 43, 56, 66,
Spirit of Norfolk, 48
Vaughan Williams, 66
Virgin Mary, 5, 14, 84
Wordsworth, 2, 9, 24

## Places
Ashwellthorpe, 31, 43, 61, 64, 69, 86, 100, 105, 109, 111
Beccles, 83
Bracon Ash, 86
Breckland, 12
Broadland, 65
Bunwell, 42, 86
Caister, 67
Cley, 8
Cringleford, 10, 70
Feltwell, 69
Fersfield, 86
Flordon Common, 16, 52, 79, 95, 106
Forncett, 86
Forncett St. Mary, 106
Fundenhall, 38, 41, 61
Gressenhall, 78
Greyfriar's Priory, 5
Hapton Hall, 32
Hempnall Churchyard, 20
Hethel Churchyard, 54
Holt, 5, 96
Horsey Mere, 46
Long Stratton, 86
Lower Wood, Ashwellthorpe, 8
Lyng, 102
Morningthorpe Churchyard, 20
Morston marshes, 77
River Stiffkey, 16, 39
River Tas, 79
River Wensum, 102
River Yare, 11, 53, 70, 92
Saxlingham Nethergate, 104
Saxthorpe, 96
Shelton Church, 20
Silfield, 86
Sistine Chapel, 36
Sparham pools, 102
Sprowston, 30
Stiffkey saltmarsh, 77
Stoke Holy Cross, 90
Strumpshaw Fen, 95
Tacolneston, 61, 86
Tasburgh marshes, 32
Tharston, 74
Thetford Forest, 100
Thursford Wood, 39
Upton Fen, 48
Walsingham Abbey, 5, 14
Wattlefield, 43
Wymondham, 10, 24, 86
Yare Valley Walk, 70

## Trees
alder, **11**, 18, 48, 52, 65, 70, 79, 92
apple, 109
ash, 3, 82, 109
aspen, 28
bark, 85
birch, 8, 102
bird-cherry, 39
bread-and-cheese tree, 23
chestnut, 85
durmast oak, 88
elder, 42, 46, 54
elm, 94, 109, 112
English yew, 16
English oak, 88
hawthorn, 13, **23**, 32, 50, 52, 60, 103
hazel, **9**, 54, 64, 82, 90, 100, 103
holly, 3, 13, 108, 109
hornbeam, 26
horse chestnut, 36
lime, 109
oak, 3, 39, 48, 78, 103, 109
palm willow, 17
pendunculate oak, 88
poplar, 92, 109
quickthorn, 23
sessile oak, 88
silver birch, 82
southernwood, 77
spindle, 60, 64, **103**
sycamore, 64, 82
willow, 70, 102, 109